D1497852

The Jew in
Early American Wit
and
Graphic Humor

Other Books by the Author

JEWS IN RELATION TO THE CULTURAL MILIEU OF THE GERMANS
IN AMERICA UP TO THE EIGHTEEN EIGHTIES
New York 1947

THE JEWS IN AMERICAN ALASKA (1867–1880)
New York 1953

THE JEWS OF CALIFORNIA
From the Discovery of Gold up to 1880
New York 1960

THE JEW IN THE OLD AMERICAN FOLKLORE
New York 1961

JEW AND MORMON
Historic Group Relations and Religious Outlook
New York 1963

JEW AND IRISH
Historic Group Relations and Immigration
New York 1966

GESCHICHTE DES NIEDEREN JUDISCHEN VOLKES
IN DEUTSCHLAND
Eine Studie über historisches Gaunertum, Bettelwesen
und Vagantentum.
New York 1968

THE GERMAN JEW IN AMERICA
An Annotated Bibliography Including Books, Pamphlets and
Articles of Special Interest
New York 1968

STUDIES IN JUDAICA AMERICANA
New York 1970

JEW AND ITALIAN: HISTORIC GROUP RELATIONS
AND THE NEW IMMIGRATION (1881–1924)
New York 1971

The Jew in Early American Wit and Graphic Humor

by

RUDOLF GLANZ

KTAV PUBLISHING HOUSE, INC.
New York
1973

Library of Congress Cataloging in Publication Data

Glanz, Rudolf.
   The Jew in early American wit and graphic humor.
   Includes bibliographical references.
   1. American wit and humor—History and criticism. 2.
Jewish wit and humor—History and criticism. 3. Jews in
the United States—Anecdotes, facetiae, satire, etc. 4. Jews
in literature. I. Title.
PS430.G5   817'.009'352   72–5819
ISBN 0–87068–189–3

Manufactured in the United States of America

55733

To Gladys Rosen
in Friendship

Table of Contents

Preface

I am indebted to Mrs. Ruth Glushanok for editorial help in preparing the manuscript.

I want to express my gratitude to the New York Historical Society and the New York Public Library for their invaluable help in the pursuing of my theme through the years and for their permission to reproduce the photographs in this volume.

RUDOLF GLANZ

Introduction

Humor consists primarily in the recognition of what is incongruous in a character or a situation, and frequently illustrates some fundamental absurdity in human conduct (leading also in some cases to pathos). It is not as intellectual as wit, which is one of its faces, and which has the quality, in speech, writing, thought, and visual art, consisting in a quickness of the perception of analogies between unlike things, sharply and briefly expressed. Wit is, above all, a product of keen consciousness, the more intensified when it takes as its target situations in human society, then becoming straight social criticism.

Traditional folklore and wit are separated, in theory, by a thin line; however, a wide gap appears when the driving force of wit is examined. Of the entire realm of traditional folklore only the proverb, that expression of the life experience of generations, comes close to wit in its satirically pointed awareness. In wit, reason takes the lead; even when criticism is not its prime aim and it thrives only through the aptness of its expression of contrasts, whether real, assumed, or imagined, reason is still its guide to laughter.

11

Literary humor is more closely related to the spirit of folklore. Its themes, especially in tales, have usually been potent in folk imagination for some time before a creative individual mind exploits them in a literary way. It is true that in folklore, fantasy roams unbridled, whereas literary conception in the humoristic tale tames the imagination.

In his way through millenia, the Jew was both a target on his own, and used as an expression of the general criticism of social conditions. He was, in addition, the subject of an unbridled folk imagination in the folklore of nations as well as in their literary and graphic humorous creations. Transplantation to the American scene was destined to test the effectiveness of previously held notions about him, and to demonstrate, using the Jew as a medium, the new things of the new continent. Often, these things were revealed through social criticism humorously expressed. Historical truth described in these new creations, through the position held in them by the Jew, throws a different light on the new American world, as well as on the old European world, so different, and so often in opposition to each other.

The cultural and social history of mankind is enriched by the research into and examination of the new role played by the Jew on the new continent.

CHAPTER 1

The Jew in Western Wit and Humor

In europe, the Jew's place in the world image of his Christian neighbors, was more or less solidly defined; he was a well-known object around which their folk imagination and social humor could wind. In literature and drama the Jew was represented as the personification of evil or, later, as a figure of comedy. The religious antagonism, long supported by church and state, which produced such folk fantasy as the legend of the Wandering Jew never radiated the same strength of feeling in America as was common in the Old World. From the beginning, the rebellious protestant sects that migrated to the New World identified themselves with the Hebrews of Biblical literature: their emphasis on the Old Testament, their attitude toward Hebrew as a holy tongue and the Hebrews as the People of the Book, led to a different image than that held by their forebears in Europe —at least on the surface. For a long time, the religious notions of the founders of the American civilization so dominated the Americans' image of the Jew that his appearance as a real member of a living contemporaneous community of people came to their consciousness only slowly and reluctantly.

The contrast between the real subjects, the Jewish people struggling for survival as a community of human beings in new times and on a new continent, and the unreal picture consisting of a mixture of the most diverse interpretations of Biblical literature, led to the wildest notions: the identification of the Indians as the Lost Ten Tribes of Israel, the importance of the conversion of the Jews as a preliminary to the redemption of the world, and continuous comparisons of various Christian sects with Judaism, all of which almost erased the real living Jew.

The separation of the Jew from his religious prototype finally came about in the American consciousness only under the pressure of the experiences gained in an America in a state of flux, turning rapidly into an urban capitalistic industrial nation after the Civil War, in which the role of the Jew became unmistakably recognizable.

American wit at the time of the build-up of this industrial society became a mirror of reality in which the Jew appears as a driving element. Bearer of an old culture, the Jew, on the new continent, worked to find success in an environment which evaluated people according to new economic categories, newly rising. At the same time, he sought to transplant the historic values of his former community to this new world. No wonder that much that was understood in him was derided in the cruel humor of the tough, young, still-to-be conquered continent; no wonder that he was often forced into a category of beliefs which could not easily be erased even by his economic rise. The Jew was here, as nowhere in his history, on strict probation . . . while an amazed environment looked on.

Nevertheless, an important difference was already manifest at this juncture compared with his treatment in Europe. Social criticism of the Jew in capitalist America, from the beginning, became identified with a measure of self-criticism within the new society as well. The popular Biblical word-image of the Golden Calf may serve as an instance of such self-criticism: Since earliest times, the Golden Calf was used in Europe as a symbol of "Jewish mammon worship." In America, however, it always represented the money principle, generally. It appears in this aspect also in the crooked mirror of laughter and as the expression, also, of the discomfort felt by individuals forced to submit their cultural ideas to this impersonal principle. Thus, the image of the Golden Calf caught hold as the self-criticism of a nascent American cultural consciousness.

To gain an inner understanding and knowledge of historical situations, although in a more indirect way, folklore is no less valuable an instrument than the wit and literary humor of the times, although admittedly, in this form it is somewhat harder to seize upon the truth. Truth in the field of wit has at its disposition a unique instrument—the caricature— which, on occasion, makes use also of the visible things of folklore, as, for example, the three balls of the pawnbroker, used as symbols in the drawings. The value of caricature as a path to historical truth should not be underestimated. Its effects are immediate and powerful. The caricaturist is able to allow fantasy to roam freely or he can exercise self-restraint for the sake of achieving specific goals. We see this best in the classic example of the political caricature, where social reality is the artist's first and unconditional intent.

The knowledge of the value of caricature and its general character were early understood in America. An announcement of 1839 proclaims:

Caricature seldom stings the faller, and never handles to obscure. Once more—the caricaturist is the best historian.[1]

Thus, by means of caricature the deeper meaning of the symbolism of the money principle, through the Jew, is demonstrated by the use of the simple formula of the Golden Calf. Over the road of the Biblical Jew, this symbol strikingly represents the most important development in America: its changeover from an agrarian, land-oriented economy to an industrialist-creating riches, for whom land was no longer the symbol, but to whom money became a new principle which could be attacked much in the same way as the earlier mammon-service of the Jew was attacked in a still religious Europe.

CHAPTER 2

The Bible People
and the Jew

Europe was inextricably attached to the historical Jew and there was no getting rid of the memories he called forth. America, however, accepting the European heritage only reluctantly or half-willingly, could, at least in its humor, imagine itself removed from these memories. The play of the imagination might take the form of a protest launched against dragging the Jewish past into the present, demanding that the forward-looking, youthful nation must set itself free from the shadows of the past. In this spirit, the protest is even carried into the nursery:

> . . . Mother, I am sick of the Jews, says he, I should think the Jews had a hard enough time a wanderin' for 40 years, it seems to me if I was in minister places I would let 'em rest a little while now and go to preachin' to livin' sinners, when the world is full of 'em. . . .[1]

The wish to be let alone should bring alleviation to a situation all too theological, and carries along the conviction, that even though difficulties might be encountered, the new world cannot in any case refer to the old Jews any more.

17

. . . I am willin' to bear any reasonable cross, mother, but I hate to tackle them old Jews and shoulder 'em, for there don't seem to be any need of it.[2]

The Biblical Jewish past was represented in American education mainly through the study of the "holy" Hebrew language which, as a part of the curriculum of American higher schools, was the crown of one's education. As the symbol of the spiritual achievement of man, the Hebrew oration made in public, was offered at the beginning or the conclusion of one's formal education. The unreality of this situation was not lost upon many Americans: a dead language speaking to the living, and was satirized in the talk of a man who had experienced in his own person the whole world of spoken languages. This is the old salt who must listen to the Hebrew oration, but would rather, in accord with his travel experiences, be listening to Chinese. Both, the bore and the bored, the young man, as the speaker, and the old captain, as the captive audience, appeal to the judgment of a wider audience, the whole of America:

The Hebrew Oration.

Some years since, at a commencement in one of the eastern states, the auditors were entertained part of the forenoon with a Hebrew oration. Being quite weary of the discourse, a person whispered (to) his companion, who was a New England sea captain, that he wished the young man, instead of facing the audience, would address himself to those that understood Hebrew. "Do you so,?" said the son of Neptune, "then by *nowns,* brother Jonathan, there would not be a single point of the compass that would suit him."[3]

Apart from the obvious anti-intellectualism of the new land, we find that the attempted indifference to the old European attitudes resulted in rationalizations which belittled the Jews even in minutiae, arriving in this case at historical criticism that proved the irrelevance and unimportance of Jewish history. On the ground of the lack of those little things which are present in the history of other peoples, a total indifference to Jewish history may be assumed:

> *Omitted facts.* You will search the history of the ancient Jews in vain for an instant of a man's clawing around in the dark after a boot-jack to throw at a cat. It is the absence of these little details that makes the history of the ancient Jews so uninteresting.[4]

This denial to Jewish history of any relevance to the needs or customs of the present, creates the feeling of American independence from the historical bonds asserted by European peoples throughout many centuries.

a. *New contact with the Bible people*

Ill humor does not hold out for long. New contact with life is found wherever new situations awaken time-honored associations of thought; thus, the long standing Biblical knowledge of the Anglo-Saxon was never abrogated. For instance, not only religious, but political and social defiance are expressed in Biblical terms:

The First Quaker.

The Indian . . . told him, that *Mordecai* was the first *Quaker*, for he would not pull off his hat to Haman.[5]

In the same way the visual pronouncement of American independence—the unfurling of the flag by Israel Putnam—may have renewed memories of Biblical battle array.[6]

Once contact was established, including the old Bible people in the daily prayer, at least, appears as a humoristic peculiarity, and tolerable as such;[7] whereas the great annoying unknown, the Hebrew language, shows up rather as an object of curiosity, the secret meaning of whose words is searched for in a New England "studded with learned societies:"

Yankee Cabala.

Old Samuel Winston, Esqu. . . . one of his notions was
Cabala. . . . Cabalistic Science is a cute arrangement of
picters, figures and letters so as tew mean suthin' and
here is an example of how sich arrangements due read. . . .[8]

However, mere contact with the history of the Bible people
doesn't create a continuum in the present. Such a state of
matters is achieved only if Bible knowledge transfers imagina-
tively the geographical map of Palestine to the American
landscape, river and place names taking on Biblical designa-
tions. The motive for the individual choice—the giving of
one of these names—very often evades research, but there are
cases where the creative act of giving a place a name passes
before our eyes and demonstrates a humoristic note.[9]

Aside from name giving, there are even situations where
the product of the Biblical landscape gains a special meaning
—Judea's vine testifies for the task of American Temperance:
"The Wine of Judea . . . was the pure juice of the grape
without any mixture of alcohol,"[10] an admonition, however
it is meant, that certainly does not lack a humorous flavor.

Compared to the numerous uses of actual Bible knowledge
in the form of literary humor, this knowledge plays only a
modest role in graphic humor. To be sure, the Golden Calf
may be worked into a caricature and, occasionally, political
personalities may appear in cartoons in Biblical personifica-
tions as, for instance, Greeley depicted as Moses and Grant
as Pharaoh.[11]

Another difference from European attitudes is perceivable
in the art of caricature where we find a complete lack of an
erotic caricature with Biblical intimations in America.
"Moses in the reeds;" Solomon in his glory, the bathing
Susannah peered at by lascivious old men,[12] all this was taboo
in an America without a sexual literature of its own and a
corresponding graphic erotic art. It is characteristic for this
Puritan nation to exclude humorous representations of Bib-

lical material even from caricatures of its own actual polygamy issue: the controversy with the Mormons. There is
not to be found among all the Mormon caricatures a real
erotic drawing, not even the famous picture of Brigham
Young's marital bed can qualify as one.[13] Incidentally, a
Biblical erotic Mormon caricature could easily have con-
tained an anti-Semitic point, following the nature of this
antipolygamy argument (the Jews demonstrated as representatives of polygamy in ancient times).[14]

CHAPTER 3

The Jew Among the Nations

T HE HUMORISTIC ASPECT of the "lost" Jewish tribes was illuminated by the forcefully visual proofs of the presence of the Jew in the midst of the European peoples. Nevertheless, knowledge about the historical Jew in his dispersion was not too prevalent, and the humorist adhered only to anecdotal material on the sufferings of the Jew or other Jewish experiences in the world. Tricks played on the Jew in the style of "How they jested in the Good Old Time" are neither forgotten nor are they set aside as the substance of new effusions of wit. Numerous anecdotes of "How the Jew was jewed" spring from this basic medieval joy about the suffering of the Jew, especially when it can be bound together with the American catchall of a bet. The Jew losing his bet (mostly by fraud) suffers not only from the inhumanity of his torturers but also as a consequence of the loss of his bet; and most often, it is the Jew's debtor who is freed from his debt by the bet won.[1] The object of the bet is preferably chosen from theological points of discussion; thus, the Jew is also the loser *sub specie aeternitatis*. The story may also be one about the Jew's worldly experiences, however, like the following, which is particularly piquant because it is told about the first Jewish Hebraist in America and deals with the intimate Christian theme, "How the Red Herring smells—" in Lenten times. The "merchant" in the story stands for "Jew" and the "Jesuit" for the American trickster, the two this time united in a conspiracy against the innocent public:

Mr. Juda Monis, who was a Jew, but embraced the christian religion and was baptized and who was a Hebrew preceptor in the college of Cambridge, Mass. 1732, would some times relate in his broken English, the following story: "Van I vas in Italy, I did know two broders, one vas a merchant, and toder vas a Jesuit. De merchant said, "broder, I has just received a cargo Red Herrings, and if you preach a sermon will make me sell my Red Herrings, I will give you something very handsome." "Yes, broder, you know *Lent* ish just by, and you may pend pont I will do for you." Next day he stept into de pulpit, and began his sermon—"Bredren, I got one, two, tre tings to say to you; you know tis our duty to keep Lent, for Moses he fast forty days . . . but more than all dat—the church says you shall keep Lent, so dat matter settl'd. But vat favor tis all dis time we keeping fast, we may eat as much fish as we mind to, else we be starved to det; but I no need say much bout dis—but of all fish, my bredren, you better eat de Red Herring; for he dat do eat great deal Red Herring, will certainly go to Heaven and dis vat I going to prove to you know. He dat does eat great deal Red Herring, will be very dry; he dat ish very dry must drink great deal of drink; he dat ish drink great deal of drink will be very drunk; he dat ish very drunk must go to sleep; he dat ish asleep cannot sin; and he dat does not sin will go to heaven." This train of reasoning one may suppose, procured a rapid sale for the *Red Herrings* and they went off *swimmingly*.[2]

Remarkably, Judah Monis is already talking in a gibberish approximating what will later be linguistically appended to the Jew in American humor; the spelling, similarly, is close to the way in which the Jew in wit and humor stories will later speak.

Nevertheless, despite the predilection for the anecdotal, an occasional excursion into the philosophy of history was not excluded. The following poem connects the fate of the Jew, in his downfall, with the decay of the other peoples around him, and lets him finally land on the same plain on which the Yankee has set his foot:

General Average.

Alas! for the ease with which races decay,
What was Absalom once is Fagin to-day.
Yet Fagin himself, that arch filcher of "wipes"
Was one of a constant succession of types,
Since Gentile and Jew, Roman, Saxon and Celt,
From glories ancestral the same lapse was felt.
. . . When Truth stepped aside, and Conscience withdrew,
To have a clear field for a Yankee and Jew.[3]

Of the more recent history of the Jew among the nations it is, then, only his performance in the mushrooming European capitalism that drew the American folk-imagination to him. The power of the medieval Shylock-image holds on as an idea, and is reflected in word usage as well as in the creation of new words and popular sayings. Very soon, however, all this is overshadowed by the Rothschild legend as the saga of the new capitalism, furnished with a special meaning for America.[4] As a hybrid of the Middle Ages and modern times, "Shylock of Frankfurt"[5] appears. In its pure state, the Rothschild legend implies a perversion of the original Shylock idea. No longer does it express the absoluteness of the personal right to money, but rather the pretension of money to be acknowledged as the universal power in the world, with Rothschild as the representative of that claim.

Thus, the appearance of the Shylock figure in American conception and speech had a deeper cultural and philosophical meaning for America itself. The rise of capitalism in the New World was felt to be inescapable and all new values formed according to its model; to the new "potentate" money, all other claims had to submit. In such a situation it was, at once a comfort and a diversion to demonstrate that lust for money and money pretension, in at least one mode and one figure, could be shown to have been overcome—and so it was that once again the Jew had to pay the bill. America could turn her face to Shylock and say: Thank God, I am not of this breed. "America is not a Shylock." In the train of this attested saying in respect to the whole American people came, the use of the Shylock-phrase by the individual being, in various situations when he found that he had a need for it.

In the Rothschild legend, American capitalism already carries its head high and free and its face open; it is the thrift of money as the life-blood of the economy which is acknowledged in this legend. By means of its manipulation, there was created a mental image connecting the Jew with capitalism in accord with the historic European example. It is obvious that an America without finance capitalism would succumb to the incitement of historical thoughts from the old world. According to these thoughts, the Jew had always been the stimulus of historical economic development as well as the expression of all social tensions arising from such developments. One cannot better demonstrate the ending of this phase—America without finance capital—in American popular consciousness than in the following satirical poem on the appearance of the Jew on the American scene. In it, a social event of the Knickerbockers is described and illuminated from all sides. The newly arrived German Jew in New York puts up in it his claim for admission to social intercourse with the native Dutch families on the ground of his money-wealth only. He is finally, after a general all-round inquiry, acknowledged as the "potentate" of a new power, i.e., of money, and admitted as such to "Society."

> All was excited now to view
> The advent of a mighty Jew;
> A very curious looking body,

As ever shaved in gold or shoddy.
So thrifty had this German grown,
Transplanted into Gotham loam,
That he had purchased, and display'd,
In spangling fustian and brocade;
A wife, and horses, and calash,
And paid for them, 'tis said in cash!
And, also, with his gold or plate,
He'd bought a right to serve the state,
At a good distance from the seat,
Of Presidential sham and cheat;
And now was ready, with his shaves,
To cut the country into halves;
And sell a moiety of't to Slidell,
His Secesh friend and traitor-idol;
Or make a dicker with the devil,
To sell the whole, for secesh evil,
Provided he shall shave the bill,
And put "de monish" in his till!
The attention of the Dutch-man drew
The movements of this "wand'ring Jew"
For notwithstanding his queer looks
The Waghorns and the Danderhooks,

. . . .
Declared him handsome, and his State,
That of a money-potentate;
Which they could scarcely praise too much,
It was so pleasing for the Dutch![6]

Chapter 4

The New Economy

U<small>SING HUMOR</small> as an instrument to mirror the American presence only serves the purpose of historical debunking. The new faith in the power of money is contrasted with the Biblical superstition of the Golden Calf:

Christian Jews.

> The Jews, as we in sacred writ are told,
> To *buy* a God, gave Aaron all their Gold—
> But Christians have become so wondrous odd,
> To heap up Gold will even sell their God.[1]

Christian society appears for this reason as united behind the new capitalism as Karl Marx had stated; the Christians had become Jews through their taking over of capitalism. But in spite of the contempt shown here, there is always felt, behind the irony, a strong relationship to the new economic principle of finance, and there is open reflection upon money, wealth, and its influence on the human character. The possibility of depicting the forming of such a character through the image of the Jew and his position in modern society and economy was felt, in popular wit, to be an elementary truth. Still, there is no concern as yet with special features of character and peculiarities of money-making copied from the Jew; at first only a general and proper philosophy of life are involved. This philosophy starts with the basic question: "What is value?" and is answered as the humorist pronounces money to be the value-forming principle of the new life. However, the voice pronouncing this response is the voice of the Jew.

a. *Value and Money*

In choosing the figure of the laughing philosopher summarizing his experiences with mankind, the possibility of mirroring American life in the image of the Jew, is already emergent. It is the Jew broker, meditating in his office, who fulfills this task. From his daily preoccupation with the financial needs of suffering humanity, the humorist shapes a philosophy of this broker's workday. This philosophy not only states the value of the money principle without any doubt, but also makes incontestable, its product, the social character it formed. Again the Christians had become "Jews," but with this difference: that after they had learned this art from the Jews, Christians didn't want to take the risk of being involved in money operations any more, this risk remaining the noble privilege of the Jew during the history of world finance:

> . . . I give advice to every tribe, but physic and de law,
> But they outwit the Jews themselves,
> For bills at sight they draw;
> We, when we lend our monish, run
> Some risk tho', 'tis is small—
> But they take all de monish, and run no risk at all.[2]

In these considerations the rogue appears summarily as the product of the value-forming retort of the money. However, finer observations on the manner in which money spoils character in individual cases are not excluded. On the contrary, the general philosophy of value serves only as an introduction, the corridor through which all the later shade-figures of money have to go when its dynamic character is revealed.

However, before value becomes objectified in money, some philosophy about the immaterial character of money is in place. It must be made clear that it can buy all kinds of objects, but is nevertheless above all ordinary qualities of merchandise. It is the final value, irrecoverable. This is best expressed by the following negative mockery which is even more drastically effective through its being dressed up as a family scene:

A sensible proof.

Miss Cohenstein: Why. Fader, he has moneysch to burn!
Cohenstein: Nonsense, mein schild! You can'd insure moneysch![3]

On the other hand, viewed as purely static, money in itself is nothing, and becomes value only by means of its dynamic quality that enables it to create additional money. In this way it is transformed into a gainful occupation—the lending of money on interest. Again fatherly instruction serves in good stead:

Son: Fader dis pook says as moneysch does not pring happiness.
Father: No, mein Sohn, It's der interest vot you gets on der moneysch vot makes you happy.[4]

The pragmatic quality of money excludes the intervention of any other, even higher world. The Puritan money-lender, asked if he, a God fearing man, is not afraid to take an interest rate of nine percent on his money, has his answer ready: The Lord views this case from sublime heights, reading the nine for a six and six percent is not so bad after all.

b. *Money as a gainful occupation.*

If it is the interest alone which creates activity of money, and the joy of life connected with it, lending money in its purest form has not, in any case, anything to do with the need of a human being for merchandise. There are, to be sure, princes of money who lend it only against a future expectation of more money. They are willing to entrust it to people who can reasonably expect to gain more money through it in their businesses. Such a money prince is led by overriding conclusions based on a firm world picture. It is not the subject the pawnbroker sees before him demanding his momentary decision to lend, but the whole man standing in front of him who asks his judgment about his person and his credit worthiness. There are in this field no vulgar principles and conditions for giving credit, all is dictated by a higher insight, trustworthiness, and personal consideration. The power drunkenness of money originates not simply from its multiplication, but primarily from the victory in psychical situations achieved by all these deliberations. Also the haggling, up and down, results here in a personal relationship to the peculiar situation:

"The Bill Broker in the time of the great panic."
Proudly and wide my signboard flies,
O'ver hard up mortals not a few;
All own my sway wo for supplies
Come to me, eve those I Jew.
My will is law, none can gainsay
What I exact, my sway is plain;
I have the cash, they must obey;
Thus in distress a king I reign.
Proudly and wide, a.c.
Now a merchant comes to me to get discount,
To take up a note "Pray what's the amount?"
"Two per cent per month, and a bonus down."
"I shall be ruined." The affair's your own.
Now another whose wife in dress
And parties had brought on distress,
Comes smiling, call's me friend,
And begs the cash I'll lend.
To my terms he must conform,
Though he fret awhile and storm;

> Oh dear! have mercy, your pity pray show!"
> Oh! Oh! Oh! Oh!
> Let's halve the bonus, and so let me go;
> Oh! Oh! Oh! Oh!
> Mercy, Mr. Broker, be mild,
> Your awful demands will drive me wild.
> But since life glides so fast away,
> While the sun shines, make hay;
> For the times so bad to day,
> Tomorrow may clear away;
> As riches our steps surround,
> Let us still seek for more;
> Nor care how our acts are crowned,
> So that we add to our store.[5]

The conviction that it is the money "Vat make Jew Christian, Christian Jew,"[6] holds true on all levels of social development. However, on the highest level where in America, too, financial capital is felt as international, the Jew is trump and all money wanders to him. He is even in the picture when an international power is in need of money power. A cartoon shows us that the truly international Roman Catholic Church cannot collect its Peter's pence in any other way than by sending Rothschild's employees for it.[7] Even as a help in the case of a catastrophe that church is advised to have recourse to Jewish finance, as in a caricature of the failure of a Catholic bank in Cincinnati, which shows Jews offering a loan to Archbishop Purcell.[8] Only in a few Populist pamphlets at the end of the nineteenth century does caricature lose the value of truth through ill humor, and reveals an antisemitic point.[9]

However peaceful the nature of finance capital may appear, the American people assumed that aggressive impulses lay hidden on its ground. Popular humor wraps these impulses in totemism, and depicts the fights inside capitalism as the work of bulls and bears whose mutual mangling awakens a feeling of helplessness vis-a-vis such natural instincts and powers. Nevertheless, the Jew is imagined as moving around on firm bottom also during these fights. Only occasionally is he disappointing in his role:

> "Why, I say, Moses . . . are you a bull or a bear? Damme, I thinks you look more like a monkey."[10]

All in all, however, the ways of finance remain avenues of reason; meaningless fights are excluded and the Jew, also, is not accused of having an interest in unreasoning struggle.

c. *Money in Security*

From the heights of speculation, where a psychological look stakes money on gain, money may step down to human lowlands where it can come up against trouble. In such situations even simple mortals become acquainted with the nature of loans. This acquaintanceship hails, however from the other side of finance, bringing them, not the joy of taking interest, but the sorrow of being obligated to pay such interest. In addition to this sorrow, they incur a new duty: to put up a pledge for the secure wandering of money on this earth. Due to developments in the private needs of their lives, therefore, all their notions of money stick to this bottom where the pawnbroker is the only recognizable figure embodying the fulfillment of money wants. For those who do not dare and do not win, and for whom money means only flight from precarious situations in life, the true princes of money don't exist at all. It is only the prince of shadow-money for them and his name is pawnbroker. Nevertheless even the mere expectation of money of this kind may bring cheerfulness, and the cartoon "At the Pawnbrokers Ball," radiates the fancy of borrowed money in its glory:

> Miss Sparklestein: dot vos a very striking gostume, Misder Loanitski. Vot character do you represendt?
> Mr. Loanitski: Dis suit vos a little idea of my own. I represendt Ready Money.[11]

Wit and caricature follow the pawnbroker from the ballroom into a full life of situations in some of which he masters, and others where he is mastered by the trickster in return—the cheater cheated—as old folklore will have it. These situations give us an opportunity also to recognize his philosophy of life and, furthermore, to learn his views of his business which harden into firm maxims in accord with which he is acting.

In American reality, the Jew was not often a pawnbroker, but this did not impede, as in the other business sphere, the mirroring of the pawnbroking business in his image. In the humorists' battle against the pawnbroker, we may see the only case where an economic function, as such, is denied. Among other accusations, the pawnbroker is reproached above all with lending money to cover unnecessary expenditures, therefore not fulfilling any necessary economic function, and whose existence thus represents the antithesis to proper popular education:

Our costly funerals.

Lend me all you can. Dad's dead, an' we're goin' to give him a bully funeral.[12]

Or, seen again from the other side, things are pawned which are necessary for the personal use of the borrower; for instance, in a drawing, the pawnbroker accepts the pawn and under the picture one can read:

Song of the camel'shair shirt.

Pawn! Pawn! Pawn! The vulgar call it "hock," and Geldstein takes the underwear and puts it in his stock.[13]

In such a case the pawnbroker's imagined self-irony gives us his conception of the customer "who is taking out his summer cloding and leaves a vinter suit instead."[14]

In the extreme mockery of the theme of the pawn accepted by the Jew, the highest comic effect is reached by letting the

"Lend me all you can. Dad's dead, an we're goin' to give him a bully funeral."

Our costly funerals (*Puck*, Vol. 6, 1879/80, pps. 508-9).

prospective borrower, who doesn't own any other object, offer his dog as a pawn. The dog is simply set on the counter of the fear-ridden Jewish pawnbroker who, in anguish, concedes the loan if only its owner would remove the animal from his store. In this way an American version of the time-worn theme "Jew and dog" is born. This is a theme used also in drawings describing other occasions, as for example, against the Jewish peddler emerging in a village. However, the pawnbroker is kingpin in his fear of the dog.

No security required.

Mr. Purple Curry: Guve me t'ree dollars on me dog.
Mr. Iky Augenstien: Mine frient, I gif you dose t'ree tollars, but I treat you as a schentlemans—I takes me no colladerals.[15]

The ongoing attack on the pawnbroker points to his untrustworthiness. Contrary to the basic agreement, made when the object is pawned, not to make personal use of it, he dresses up in the pawned clothes, rings, watches and chains, and finances the dandy appearance of his son in the same way without expense to himself.

Drawings of social events where the pawnbroker's son shows up, as at the race track, in his whole elegance of pawned equipment, while the owner of these pieces, having come to the store to redeem the pledge has to wait for the return of the young Jew dandy, become popular. "Shacob knew" is the essence of these recriminations because, ostensibly, the pawnbroker, alone in his store, cannot find the objects and has to wait for his son who is more at home in the store. On special occasions, however, when, for instance, the pawnbroker goes on summer vacations, it pays to close the shop and, dressed up in the best pawned pieces, to take himself off to the summer resort:

Levy's out!

The Catskill Mountains are full of Jews.—Daily Paper.
Go Isaac, and put the shutters up,

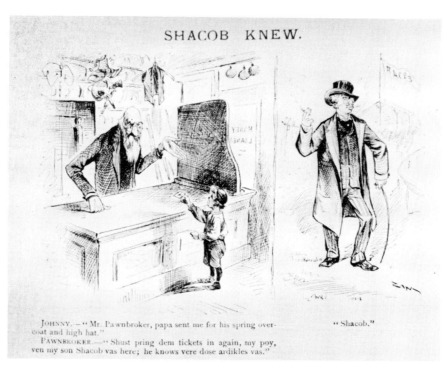

Shacob knew *(Puck,* Vol. 17, 1885, p. 356).

And take the three balls down;
V'eel stop the pizziness for a' veek,
Und go us oud of town.
For tings was very tull shust now,
Und gustomers was few,
So you und mudder und meinself
Vill go dose Gadskills trough.
The Cohens and the Rosenbaums,
The Solomons and Steins,
Are through those mountains, down and up,
And having sholly dimes.
Vee'l wear our gustomers' di'mond rings,
Deir chains and vatches too.
Dont shute of glo'es ve last took in,
Vill shust apout with you.[16]

The pawnbroker's sign, the three balls, in themselves already one of the rare instances of drawn folklore in America, had seen better days when it was used for more cheerful occasions, viz, to mark the presence of taverns. With the ongoing years, by the time the nineteenth century was reached, the three balls had acquired their fixed position as a symbol for loans on pawns on the new continent as well. Wit and humor was always on hand, orally or through use of the slate pencil, to render, by use of this symbol, the key to eminent situations of social life, in this way endowing a real joke-idea with deeper meaning.

In its crudest use the three balls serve to signalize the pawnbroker himself, for instance in a caricature where "The original Jacobs"[17] sits under a business sign with three balls of glass. But not only do they appear over his businessplace, they accompany him wherever he goes. The traveling pawnbroker boarding a ship with his son has them painted on his travel-bag.[18] The basic idea of this caricature is, that the ill spirit on which this type of business is founded doesn't restrict itself to the locality used for it, but goes with the pawnbroker into his private life. The same idea is expressed by another meaningful drawing: a walking stick, on which the three balls are worked together in the stick's handle.[19] It goes without saying that the three balls are painted also on the pawn ticket, suggesting a humorous *Ersatz* for the pawned objects missed direly by their owner.[20]

American humor, as far as the Jew is its target, demonstrates with favor the basic ideas of its mockery by transplanting them from the grown-up to the world of the Jewish child. In this way, not only are these ideas laughed off effectively, but the carrier of these ideas, the humoristic subject, is mocked at in his function as an educator. In the propagation of the imagined values of the pawnbroker, the educator appeals for the moment not to the stuff of ideas, but to the fantasy of the child. The three drawn balls swim in the air; they had become real airborn balloons.[21] However, if the situation becomes serious, the child is given a real visual education:

Educational.

Little Isaac: Popper, vot for you have dose three balls ofer der front door?

Lowenstein: Oh, dot vas for der benefit of dose who couldn't read; it shows vat my inderest is every month.[22]

d. *Money as a symbol*

Where money continuously guides the thoughts, there has to be a symbol that represents it and shortens the thinking process to a considerable degree. The moneyman doesn't think in hard gold but in figures and, even before figures form, this symbol is present and ready, shortening the process of figuring, as well. The caricaturist fell upon the dollar sign itself as this symbol and worked it into drawings in various ways. In all these drawings, the Jew's journey on the road to capitalism (read: America's heading straight into it) is mocked.

The first step in creating a symbol is the representation of a state of businessmindedness by the dollar sign. Furthermore, in classical imitation of older European antisemitic

THE CODFISH EXODUS TO EUROPE.

The Codfish exodus to Europe *(Puck,* Vol. 6, 1879/80, p. 178).

samples in which "eyeglasses" are chosen as book titles,
American caricatures appear where the Jew has the dollar
sign painted on his eyeglasses.[23]

In the refined form of this thought it is not the spectacles
which are at fault, but the vision of the man who can see
only the smallest figure at the bottom of the oculist's eye
chart:

> Oculist: Now tell me how many of these can you see?
> I can see noddings but the one at the bottom. (On the
> bottom of the table the dollar sign is placed.)[24]

The artist becomes a moralist demonstrating the fall of
man through the ways of money: the snake, oldest symbol
for man's fall, puffs up to become the form of the dollar
sign.[25] He further castigates the low taste of the nouveau
riche by designing a piece of furniture for the parlor in the
shape of the dollar sign.[26] In this way it becomes perfectly
clear what the Jew has before his eyes even during the time
he spends away from his business. The paradox of putting
a reclining chair in which to rest in the home of the Jew
under this sign should be noted, because in this way the
restlessness of the Jew is also intimated.

The final step takes the humorist and caricaturist into the
realm of education, this time to show us how the Jew im-
plants the value of this symbol into his children. In the
caricature "Instructive exercise" the father "Mr. Geldheimer"[27] shows up at the athletic club and directs his
children in a gymnastic exercise on a climbing pole which is
drawn in the shape of the dollar sign.

e. *Language symbols for money*

However meaningfully the caricaturist may work up his
symbol, he reaches a limit set by the visual character of his
medium where the eye cannot see any further. With language, however, it is different. Not only does language reach

Jew and Oculist *(Life,* Vol. 25, 1895, p. 239).

what the ear can hear, but also anything man can associate
with thought; therefore, also, anything the thought of money
can call forth.

First of all there are the names: The humoristic name
undertakes to characterize the main feature of an individual's
life, and a name taken from money best characterizes the
life of a capitalist. *Geldstein, Geldheimer* are only the most
obvious, simplest forms; both are modeled upon the example
of typical German Jewish names. The innumerable branches
of related forms of money names reach actually any phase and
shade of the capitalist's activities.[28] In humorous verbal use,
in addition, the word *Jew* is made available to mean simply,
the taking of interest on money loans: "jew in one year arter
that." And the word serves also to set the date on which
interest shall be due:

> Watty, my dear b'loved son, pripar tu pay two hundred
> dollars 'bout the fust ove October, fur hit'ill be jew jis'
> then. . . .[29]

The whole movement of money is thus brought, umbrella-
wise, under this notion, the moneylending Yankee himself,
"old Jeremiah Jenkins, the Jew"[30] also no longer able to
escape this fate.

f. *Commodity and price*

There comes a moment when a transition takes place in
human thinking: the abstract idea of money is transformed
into a material substance. Again, all substances of which one
can think, insofar as they enter the provenance of money,
become an abstract notion, viz. commodity.

The humorist who executes this tricky thinking process in
substitution for the simple minds, shows us first money as a
self-fulfilling purpose without relation to the things that are
measured by its increase as the only yardstick. Things in
themselves change only insofar as their change is expressed

through the yardstick of money. Quality of things becomes a measured percentage.

The meaningful humoristic dressing-up of this thought is given form in the image of angling, which is already in the people's lore, the symbol of the big chance to catch all the variety of nature. Like elsewhere the Jew is demonstrated as a meditating being, the scene becomes a pastime in his hours of rest; father and son share in it and the measurement taken appears as an act of education:

Fin and Finance.

Aby: How you tells ven you geds a bite, Popper?
Feldheimer: Der line goes down a liddle.
Aby: How much?
Feldheimer (abstractedly): Aboud one unt a helluf per cend.

At last, however, there is no escape from objective quality and things have to be measured according to their objective value, one against the other. The philosophical neophyte tries generalities first:

Gold and Corn.

. . . beautiful contrast between the gold of California and the gold of agriculture. . . . It expands to a vigorous stalk. . . . It arrays itself more glorious than Solomon. . . .[32]

However, general comparisons still don't create firm relationships between things, the gold of the corn on the stalk has first to become "commodity" to take a price expressible in money. All things together as commodities form the economic world in which it is given to man to establish relations between things and effect changes, to create prices and to let them fluctuate; this activity is business. The Jew, introduced by the humorist as the representative of the new American business, appears at the same time as the manipulator of prices on the scale of money, whose ups and downs

he calls forth by his movements. Again, however, these movements are not purely mechanical; insofar as they intend to
change the value of things, they use psychology to motivate
the buyer for this purpose. The cartoon "A useful accom-
plishment; or the beauty of swelling a customer's head,"[33]
shows the Jew reading the glorious future of the buyer of
a hat from the lines of his palm. The hat bought and much
too big before the palm reading starts, finally fits the customer's swollen head, blown up as the result of the high life
expectations indicated in his palm.

Or nature itself can, without respect for psychological
motives, bring into existence a movement upwards on the
price pillar. This is shown to us in two Jewish caricatures:

1.) A pedlar did start out one morning his stock of old
    sponges to sell;
2.) But the rain began falling in torrents, and oh! how
    those sponges did swell.[34]

In the eyes of the humorist, all other movements of
commodities on the price barometer appear to the observer
as mystical and without apparent cause. He undertakes the
task of interpreting them only in connection with other business and worldly features of the Jew. Where there is no
clue in business, price formation sinks into an abyss:

Halaf a Tollar.

Gilhooly went into Mose Schaumburg's store, on Austin
Avenue, to buy an umbrella. Mose showed him two kinds
of umbrellas, which looked very much alike, one of which
was a dollar and the other a dollar and a half. Gilhooly
examined them *critically,* and asked: "What is the difference between them?" "Halaf of a tollar," responded
Mose.[35]

Fixed prices, pillars—the comparison with the Biblical
pillar of fire then in vogue—cease being leaders in the price
desert as soon as they begin to fluctuate, then permitting the

ON A MADISON AVE. CAR.

A PLEASANT SOCIAL CHAT ON THEIR WAY TO BUSINESS.

WE CALL IT an old-fashioned Winter, probably, because, like everything else of the good old times, it is confoundedly uncomfortable.

A FIN DE SIÉCLE VALENTINE.

Phyllis, you 're one in four hundred,
No maiden with you can compare :
You are an up-to-date girl. Why ?
Because you are my world's fair !

Ogden Warde.

On a Madison Avenue streetcar *(Puck*, Vol. 32, 1892/93, p. 401).

45

comparison with the barometer. Part of the enjoyment of business, consists in the fact that prices are not fixed and that the barometer is manipulated. Of the Jew it is said that he enjoys this possibly as his secret happiness. Such a legend of price formation can, perhaps, be read into the name of "Mose Schaumburg." For him prices, instead of being a firm structure—as indicated in the "burg" ending of his name— are foamed up, although he should—according to his name *Mose*—be going after the steady pillar of prices like his Biblical namesake after the pillar of fire.

As against the trusts' system of leading to formation of prices by agreement between competitors, the manner of free price formation—whatever the traffic can bear—is held high:

An exceptional line.

Isaacs: Sooner or later dere vill be a trusd in all kinds of peezness.
Cohen: Not in der old clothes peezness. If dere vos fixed brices in dot line half der fun of it vould be gone.[36]

However, the new objectivity is already on the march. "Cheap" alone cannot satisfy the possibilities of an unchained economy any more. There is need for insight into basic motives, different from the motive for making a price "cheap." Such motives originate for the sake of the business itself. The world is driven by the necessity to do business. The Jew must stand for the purity and nonadulteration of this principle—the absolute necessity of business, untouchable in itself. Like "art for art's sake" must business be nothing but business:

Both in search for information.

Ikey: Who vos it dot said "peezness is peezness?"
His father: I don't know, Ikey. I vould like to know who efer said it vosn't.[37]

CHAPTER 5

Business

Business includes all activities involved in the process of profit-making in the form of money. American humor eagerly catching sight of these activities, uses them, even if they are far from being typical. In the fact that humor is thinking far in advance, and even hurrying ahead, of its time, lies the peculiarity of the situation; it is letting you feel, somehow, its absurdity as a mirror of the overpowering natural forces of the new continent. A statement made as early as 1864 already formulated this basic quality:

> The peculiarities of American humor as distinguished from that of the rest of mankind lies in its extreme breadth and strength of absurdity, and its powerful presentation of ludicrous images to the mind's eye.[1]

Such bigness of absurdity in the the field of business, where the natural instincts of man do not lag far behind the physical forces of nature, surely lies in the early (1844) description of an imagined lawyers' meeting with a Jewish pawnbroker as the chairman. Although the imagined scene is in England, the pronounced principles of business are

47

conceived of as fully valid in America; this at a time when lawyers as a class had only recently had its start there in undertaking to achieve social status. It goes without saying that all their deliberations are given in the language imputed to the Jew. And the humorist is especially eager to make this idiom useful for philosophical expression too:

> Shentlemen's of the Shvell Mob—Let's come to pishness; ve all like pishness—dere's notin' like pishness. Ma heart's is pishness. . . .
> De vorld, vich vos made out of notin', makes notin' of you; but if you make sometin' out of de vorld, vy, vell and goot—it will show you have de pest of de vorld; and isn't getting de pest of de vorld vot every von tries for? (Loud cheers). Vot is a man thought of who has de vorst of de vorld? Is he not called a fool vid no pluck, no prains, no talons, no genus, no tac, and vorse and vorse, no *monish?* Vell, den, de vay is to get de *monish,* for de vorld say, you don't get der *monish,* you don't get any ting from de vorld? . . .[2]

The principle remains, always, the same even if the human being transfers from one business to another. It makes no difference if the story is told about the money-lender in Venice or is reported as a pork-story on one of the new rich in Porkopolis:

The meat-merchant of Venice.

> . . . This Shylock evidently feels that business is business, and that even if a banker at an advanced age chooses to depart from his regular line and go into the meat trade, the principle holds good.[3]

On the summit of life's success stars revolve around one another and, at a given moment, free choice may decide which one is to be elected as the leading star, and which merely as a satellite. For politics revolves around business and, then again, politics may just mean big business:

His choice.

Mr. Isaacs: Mein Sohn, vich would you radder haf, if some von offeredt to gif it to you, seat in der United States Senate or a seat in der Stocks Exchange?
Isaacs Junior: Vhy, a seat in der Senate, Fader; it gosts more![4]

If one's view is concentrated on the power of wealth, comic comparisons between old established wealth and the riches of the self-made new arrivals from the immigrant classes, cannot fail to make an appearance, and humor quickly gives the decision to the new arrivals:

Dominant races.

Isaacs: You t'ink der Anglo Saxons vos going to rule der eart'?
Cohenstein: Vell, mey be dey mighd, but dot von't brevent der Hebrews from owning id![5]

In this way the advantage the old established rich have over the new is reduced to one item: Their forefathers were already in America when the nation's great sons made history; for the new rich, who were not there, it is naturally interesting to learn how money was made in the olden times:

Getting down to business.

Grabbenstein, Jr. (reading from schoolbook)—"in 1776, Washington, Adams, Hancock, and Jefferson were among those who were making history—
Grabbenstein, Sr. (taking book)—Is dere a list of der men, or firms, who vere making moneysh dose times?[6]

In the above example, the implication is that the great men of history were opposed to the founders of the big American fortunes. In the same way also, for the present time, the quality of making history is compared with the ability to do business. Thereby it is imputed that also at the time of historic events the latter role better suits the Jew:

Different makes.

Wogglebaum: Did you hear dot young Ikey Levy hass gome back? He has been mit Dewey in Manila Bay making history!
Burnstein: Vouldn't it been better if he had stayed in Baxter Bay making moneysch?[7]

The Jewish sailor, shown in the illustration for this joke, leaves no doubt in the beholder that the theme, "Heroes and merchants" existed well before the days of the First World War.

As an eminently practical business, making money doesn't tolerate any other gods other than itself:

Carrying coals to Newcastle.

Canvasser: I'd like to show you this book, "How to Get Rich."
Mr. Isaacs: Mein frendt, I haf no time to read dot book. I spend all my shpare time tryin' to find oudt how to maig money.[8]

With such a concept of business as the ideal, a potential preparedness to conclude a deal must always be held in readiness. This preparedness serves as an eye-opener; therefore a man may easily be awakened from sleep if an opportunity for business is at hand:

> Mr. Aaron Levy, a gentleman of the Jewish persuasion, was sleeping soundly on board a ship that had become disabled. Suddenly he was awakened by the cry, so welcome to all else on board, of "A sail! a sail!" Jumping up from his berth, forgetful for the moment of his whereabouts, the ruling passion strong in death exhibited itself in the auctioneers' cry: "A sale! a sale! Where? where? Put it off, whatever you do, until I've got my catalogue ready."[9]

To call forth the special occasion is also admissible. In the following, we may easily recognize a scene of a later Chaplin movie:

There was a Dear, Nice Benevolent Old Hebrew Gentle-
man who attracted considerable attention on the East Side
of town lately by giving away base-balls to the small boys—
But it was noticed that the dear, nice benevolent old
Hebrew gentleman always appeared the next day with a
"Glass-put-in" outfit, and did a rushing business.[10]

Other occasions may consist in getting commodities for
nothing, i.e., on credit, without intending to pay as is demonstrated by a "deal" of that kind:

pargains. Vot vas der brice?
Cohenstein: I didn't asgk; I got them at sixty days![11]

Thus the old wisdom that four borrowed dollars are of
better use than two presented as a gift is confirmed. The
reason: It is a thousand pities for the two dollars lost in
between.

The natural course of matters propelled by business can
generally not be anticipated by trickery; thus, the Jew is not
free from fear of economic crisis as he is shown in this
situation:

How's trade?

Oh, mine heavens! bad.[12]

There is no question any more about personal well-being.

There must, in the end, be a limit in the finite world, to
the maneuvering in all directions for business. Even if the
Jew is not terrified by theories of money and crisis, he has
to recognize that there are natural boundary lines in every
country:

A sorry outlook.

Levy: Der Jews are rapidly monopolizing all der peezness
off der country.
Isaacs (sadly): Ach, yes! soon dere vill pe nobody left dot
ve can shtick![13]

Contrasted with the dark forebodings and prognosis is, in the long run, always an active optimism and urge to betterment. As the right concept of life this is once again shown in an educational scene:

Business is business.

We must begin and cut down our oxpenses, Jakey.
Vat for, Fadder? Pizzness is goot.
Yah, Jakey. And we must make it a leetle petter![14]

Well-conceived rationalism is inimical to extravagance. Nevertheless, an extraordinary situation may justify a sacrifice if thereby a way is opened to some high ambition. In the caricature "A world grabber," the vision of a distant chance is made vivid:

Cohenstein: Mine frendt, vere are you from?
Chinaman: From Hong Kong, China.
Cohenstein: Mine frendt, take dot for a kervorter! I vill lost monish, but I vant to get der China trade![15]

a. *The customer*

As a counterpart of the man clinging to business, appears the comic figure in the business spectacle, the customer. The treatment he gets in life is the consequence of his psychological needs; but the lessons drawn from this treatment are summed up in abstractions, and represent again a fit object of family education. It goes without saying that preference is given here to visual instruction; instances seen, however, include not only the mastering of the customer through the Jew, but also examples of independent thinking on the part of the objects of this education in the family circle.

Wherever the customer is introduced by the humorist, it appears that the Jew is continuously thinking of him, if he is not just thinking of himself, or just because he is thinking of himself.

The customer has thus come into view as a being of uncommon importance, in fact as the only human factor in business and actually the only one that is to be considered at all.

A powerful saint.

Jim Hickey: Are there any saints in the Jewish calendar, Isaacs?
Isaacs: Ja; vun—Ein Gustomer—![16]

For him the businessman hurries mentally through the whole continent, symbolizing in this way the scope of the Jewish economic sphere. As so many other things relevant to the customer service of the Jew, this can best be illustrated in the clothing store and its assortment:

The right shop.

Customer: I want to git a mixed suit; what hev ye got in that line?
Proprietor: I haf pants from Pensalvania; I haf vests from Vest Virginia; I haf collars from Colorado; I haf coats from Dakota; I haf neckties from Connecticut! Mixed suits vas my specialty![17]

The friendly jokesmith who formed Pennsylvania from the "sale" of the "pants," will, by mixing states in a mixed suit, also express the admixture of the Jew to all social aggregates of the country. Thus, he even risks ordering "coats" from Dakota which would better have had them delivered there instead. In spite of all these illogical details the "mixed suit" fit well, because it fit the popular notion of the Jew.

Not only in physical space is the Jew ready to undertake to travel far for his customer. He does it also in the mental dimension of figures which he measures in new price markings. The traces of these measuring activities are lasting:

Always ready.

Customer: The suit is all dusty.
Shomberg: Ah, mein vrent, dot gomes from der chalk
vere we marks dem down so often.[18]

In many Schaumburg stories, the German Jewish name of
the seller was fitted to a Texas background. It served as one
branch of a widely ramified humoristic expansion of the
figure of the typical German Jewish immigrant, risen to the
position of a successful merchant. Here a new remarkable
element begins to play its role, the forming of adequate
names for the Jewish figures in American wit and humor.
With the development, as a social class, of the German Jewish
immigrants it is the "heimers" and the "steiners," who are
viewed as their representatives. It is announced that where
the "heimers" are, the "steiners" will follow soon. We are
met by a broad knowledge of the formation of German names
as, for instance, the fancy name "Cohnheim"; it is felt, in
a way, that the Jew imagines Germany to be the land where
a "Cohn" has a real home. A list of all representative
humoristic names of joke figures from the German Jewish
social class, line up by themselves through the themes of
these jokes. Only the newer Jewish immigrant class from
Eastern Europe creates basically new Jewish humoristic
names. It may be assumed, as a rule, that the suffix "—ski" in
the name characterizes the Eastern European Jewish milieu
from which a joke type hails. In this way, names of pure
humoristic fantasy are constructed which are derived from
the activity of the human type, for instance "Misfitski" for the
Jewish tailor who makes bad clothes.[19] This is very different
from the genuine names of German Jews in humoristic use,
which may be real at least in one aspect, and fantastic only
by connotation. (There are real Cohnheims in existence but
a place as indicated by the name, does not exist in Germany.)
The genuine name, Cohnheim, is therefore put to shame by
all the other —"heimers" who come from existing places that

ONE OF THE FAMILY.

ROSENSTEIN.— Let me sell you a suit, mein frient — you look splendid in it ven you go to dot Methodist church on Sunday!

PASSER-BY.— I don't go to the Methodist church. I'm a Swedenborgian.

ROSENSTEIN. — Come right in — dose Switzenbergers vas first cousins oft mine — I gif you a bargain!

One of the family (*Puck*, Vol. 32, 1892/93, p. 396).

their names display, like Oppenheim, Mannheim, and even Dinkelspiel—who are introduced faithfully into American wit representing their birthplaces.

In our case of a travel through the realm of price figures, the German Jewish *Bargainbaum* serves first and is, in some distance of time, followed by the Eastern Jewish Markdown-ski.[20] Continuation of the trip leads to lower regions. The humorist is eager to show us that the pillar of buying desires rises when the price pillar sinks. The deepest longing of the Jew is, thus, only the *"Cheap;"* quality merchandise is out of the question. Even the birds in the trees sing out this truth, and this time the discovery is made by Junior and is transformed into an act of educating the older generation:

> Abraham: Vere vos you all dis day?
> Ikey: Fadder, I vos in de woods, an' I saw a nest full of young burts, and dey did nothin' but sing "Cheap. Cheep!"
> Abraham: Mine cracious, Ikey! get all dem burts you can! I'll hang dem in der frond window and let dem holler 'bout de goots.[21]

The use of living nature in the world of prices lives on, the memory of those, however, who have discovered the "Cheap," lives beyond their lifetime as we are shown by a thoughtful cenotaph:

> Young Abrahams had been brought up to consider "trade" an institution, and a new wrinkle in that line as something that must eventually entitle the lucky discoverer to a cenotaph—said cenotaph to be built in the form of an immense and almost endless succession of hats, placed one on top of the other, with the simple legend crowning the whole—"sheap"![22]

To remain true to one's principle is to earn the admiration of posterity. Even when it only concerns a sale at "sacrifice prices" a Biblical image alone can demonstrate the greatness of the decision:

ESTABLISHING CONFIDENCE.

Establishing confidence *(Puck,* Vol. 25, 1889, p. 250).

Abraham's sacrifice.

Entire Stock of Clothing of Isaac a. Co's at a sacrifice By
Abraham.[23]

The lack of dependability in the price asked for an article
remains a favored theme of wit, especially when lowering
the price is simply a maneuver of competition:

Competition the life of trade.—Goldberg.

Say, Ikey, Bloomingstein is having a big bargain sale; you
just take those fifty-cent cards, draw a line through them,
mark them thirty-seven, and put them on the twenty-five-
cents goods. We must keep abreast of the times.[24]

The movement of prices is described as a mystery, only
occasionally dammed up. For instance, if the farmer, in spite
of rising prices, hesitates to deliver his cattle to the stockyards,
the purchase of clothing is proposed to him and clothes are
praised as the rock of price stabilization:

Meat vas gone up; but don't you gif it avay. I sell you
a bair of bants just de same brice as before.[25]

To guide him in the labyrinth of prices, the customer may
occasionally be enlightened on the basis of them all:

A loss.

Isaacstein (pathetically): Ach! mine frendt, ven I sell you
dot suit for five tollars I'm losing moneysh on it.
Farmer: You be?
Isaacstein: Yes, mine frendt;—it's *insured* fer more dan
dot![26]

Having revealed the elements of pricing intelligently to
the customer, the humorist proceeds to the slippery level of
merchandise and its special qualities. On this plane the
customer has to prove himself without the help of any expert

guidance. Occasionally, a person otherwise unsuspecting in this field, has a brain wave:

Too much of it.

Mosenstein (as Jack *tries on the four-dollar overcoat):* Dhere, mein frient, you see it don't take much money to make a shentleman of you!
Poor Jack: Yes, old man; but don't you think my gentility is a little too long in the sleeves?[27]

Excessive largeness is interpreted as an additional service to the customer:

Liberal.

Legge: Look here! I'm afraid these trousers are too big.
Cohen: Vell, I makes no extra charge for dot; I was villing to gif full measure.[28]

Generally, however, the customer's imagination is the measure of things, and they stretch according to his imagination. The seller's position becomes elastic like the merchandise he has to offer; at the same time this merchandise serves to symbolize all the extensible elements, the arbitrary change in the conception of fitting in the realm of apparel; for instance, as in the following sale of gloves:

Very accommodating.

Customer (to *Young Israelite):* Are these gloves elastic?
Israelite (decisively): Dese glofes vill do votever you vants'm to do. If you vants 'em to str-r-retsh dey vill str—retch, and if you don't vants' 'm to str-r-retch dey vill dr-r-raw up an' fit close to de han'[29]

If the subject of misfitting merchandise was utilized to evoke laughter through its silliness, serious conflict was only to be averted by the presence of mind of the seller, as in the story of the sale of a pair of boots to a soldier:

He had walked only one or two squares, however, when the soles came off! Of course he at once made tracks to the Jew store, and on entering accosted him with "Look here, you scoundrel, you've swindled me. These boots ain't worth a cent!" The Jew looked up in amazement at his customer, and putting on an air of well-feigned astonishment, replied:
"Oh, dem ish not infantry poots: I thought you was a cavalry man."[30]

Occasionally the comic effect is not reached predominantly by the aptitude of the Jew as a seller, but, on the contrary, by having him come up against a shrewd opponent in the game. This opponent plays a trick on the seller, sometimes even running away with the tried-on, unpaid-for suit. In the following case the joke's variety is reduced to a mere out-doing in trickery by a counter-ability to sell, the object offered for sale being the Lost Tribes in book form:

Hosenstein's Error.

Hosenstein: Come in, my friend.—I sell you der lofeliest suit ohf glothes you efer saw!
Stranger: One moment, please—allow me to sell you a copy of this magnificent work "The Lost Tribes of Israel!" richly illustrated, only two dollars and seventy-five cents![31]

We learn little from the humorist about the Jew as a customer in real life. Here is a case of wildly capricious fantasy, representing an adaptation of English humor, where the pardoned Jew is introduced as a customer:

He waited to see if he could bargain with Mr. Ketch for the other gentleman's clothes.[32]

b. *The store*

The store of the Jew is the locale indispensable to the humor of otherwise abstract and purely psychological things as, for instance, estimating the value of objects, establishing their prices, and mastering the customer. In the concept of the store, old and new notions meet. First, is the memory of medieval times when, traditionally, all the treasures of the world were pawned at the Jew's who worked them over, thus bringing to the imagination an image of the store as an alchemist's laboratory or as a hell's kitchen; this is linked with the delusion of the Jew in relation to modern gold and genuine jewelry with diamonds, brought from distant places. And finally, there is the mass product of modern manufacture, ready-made clothing, followed by gold-plated junk jewelry appearing hand in hand with the newest in window displays and advertising ideas. It may be said that the old "magic" concept of the Jew who furnishes the treasures, lives on still in the false glamor of a new time, and that in the store more peculiarities of the Jew show up than in all the other themes of humor; on the other hand, window display and psychological advertising of the new American world, demonstrate the inescapable new ways of a modern economy.

The demoniac element of the store is further illuminated in that the shop of the Jew actually offers everything imaginable according to the analogy of the devil's workshop. It is a storehouse of merchandise heaped up by the evil greediness and desires of human beings, delivering themselves through these evil desires to the devil. In the following early literary sample (1808), the basic idea of the origin of the Jewish store through the misguided desires of the Gentiles, is described not only in the chosen form of a business advertisement, but also in numerous local pronouncements:

> Moses Mordecai and Co. inform their friends and the world, that they have opened their Universal Ware and General Business Office, at the sign of Noah's Ark, No. 777, Mount Ararat, Salem, where they tender their services in every possible business whatever. They have now opened, and for sale or barter, a great variety of horses, ships, notes of hand, bonds (with or without mortgages),

bankchecks, shares in all the principal banks and insurance companies, current and uncurrent and counterfeit
money, ditto assorted for shaver's and brokers' use; lottery
tickets, Ohio scrip and Georgia lands by the large or small
quantity. Flour, do of sulphur, gunpowder, patriotic
resolutions, town meeting speeches and arguments of every
description, . . . newspaper communications and etymol-
ogies of words, "from the German of" R.U.U.B.—Also,
just received, by the last arrival from Germany, a small
quantity of excellent table Dumpficht, which (being a
little *dampish*) will be sold cheap.
. . . The Public Humble Servants,
    Moses Mordecai a. Comp.
    at the Sign of the Ark, No. 777 Mt. Ararat, Salem.[33]

In a medieval picture of a social scene in a knight's castle,
the Jew, with his pointed hat, stands in the corner to indicate
that this illustrious view is made possible only by the Jew's
furnishing of all the good things in the picture. In the same
way, consciousness of high social rank is dampened by the
present memory of the realities of the economic world:

The Marquis von Barraille. . . .

His resources were completely exhausted, every trinket has
been put in requisition—his gold snuff box, his diamond
ring, even his sword, as he said, had been pledged to the
brokers or pawned to the Jews.[34]

Naturally, high comic effects are brought about by clothing
this relationship of the Jew to merchandising in Biblical
clothes, and by expressing it in images known to all—in the
language of the images of the Bible:

My frends, sed he, keep my mantle out ov the hands uv
the Jews. Where is the Elisha who'll wear it?[35]

The mere nearness of the Jew to merchandising may call
out comic effects even if only minor details are depicted. For
versatility, his turning to all the possible objects of trading

The Rivals (*Life*, Vol. 26, 1895, p. 221).

of the moment may be stressed, or the advertising of wares and enticing of the buyer may be laid bare in respect to the human incentives to buy:

> What can I shell you today, mine frent. Tont say norting at all. S'elp me goodness, we've just opened a shplendid lot of fine shirts for Quakers! Shtep in and look![36]

In this instance, the customer should be moved by the tradesman's familiarity with his circumstances. However, there are cases where heroic adventures are undertaken, and the adventurer is forced to buy his necessities from the Jew before he can venture out into the distant world: "The Major, in anticipation of the prospective icebergs and frozen thermometers, bulls the flannel-market, and depletes the stocks of Isaacs Ben Levi,"[37] and we see this also in a drawing. That there is only one step from the pathetic to the ridiculous, in this case to the store of the Jew, is made apparent to us:

> Damphool . . . sold his watch to a "blaspheming Jew" to raise money with which to procure an ascension robe.[38]

Clothes and the clothing trade, with new or second-hand clothes, are used to symbolize Jews in business because of the comprehensibility of this idea to everyone. The Jew as a broker and the Jew of the stock exchange are highly bred exemplars of a species not ordinarily encountered by ordinary people. Popular wit did not neglect the opportunity of pointing at them as the highest species of the Jewish businessman but to embrace the mass-consumption audience of humor more frequently met and more easily identifiable types had to be shown: Jews met readily, without toil, whom everyone could see at certain localities where they did business. Certain experiences with them had to have at least a modicum of credibility to be able to affect those who had not yet had these experiences. The second-hand clothes

Nervy Nat and the two hundred *(Judge,* Vol. 47, 1904, No. 27, p. 3).

dealer, sometimes the peddler, but in all cases the pawn-broker, correspond to these expectations. In the clothing business the frequency of these experiences together with the variety of the merchandise accomplishes the purpose of the humorist: chic and à la mode or Old-fashioned and second-hand, made to order or ready-made, wearing well or shoddy. Insofar as the Jew enters this picture, his role may be explained also from the viewpoint of socio-economic history.

Manipulation, with clothing as an object of business, was comparatively new on the American continent. Homespun and pioneer apparel was a part of a home economy; in the cities, the clothes "which make people" were imported from England. The arrival of tailors, trained in London, or of furriers, who are apt to work directly for the customer's needs, is a frequently announced item of business advertising. That clothes could even be produced en masse for a market was an overwhelming novum for the American population, which had just been subjected to the sight of the transition of an itinerant tailor into an owner of a workshop in the established settlements. In accord with the psychological presuppositions of this change, there was talk of an invasion of the new continent by ready-made clothing. This invasion was associated in the popular consciousness with the new class of immigrants who had achieved it, the Jews. Even where the role of the Jew is recognized as progress, this invasion is an object of popular humor; jokes tell about the "mission" to clothe America and the aptness of the new "missionaries" to do this job. That, however, serious observers thought essentially in a similar manner, we see from a statistical study on Cincinnati in 1851. There, the religious and cultural life of the Jews is finished off in a few words, whereas their clothing industry is elaborated on as their real domain:

Clothing manufacturers.

This is a very extensive business here, which is principally engrossed by the Israelites of Cincinnati. One hundred

A close call for Mr. Rosenbaum *(Puck*, Vol. 32, 1892/93, p. 101).

and eight stores and shops employ 950 hands at their
work-shops. More than 9000 women work at their own
houses, for these establishments. Value of product one
million nine hundred and fortyseven thousand 500 dollars;
raw material 60 per cent. There are six establishments
alone, in the City, which manufacture more than half a
million of dollars of clothing. Cincinnati is the mart for
ready-made clothing, for the whole South and West.[39]

However, it was not so much this productive activity of
the German Jewish immigrant that stuck to the popular
consciousness, but rather its contrast, all the conceivable
phases of trading clothes in which the customer was in
direct contact with the Jew. If the literary satire of this time
is taken as a yardstick, a Jewish clothing store must have
been established in every third dwelling of Cincinnati.
Basically different from the European role of the Jew in the
clothing trade, there was, in America, no sweeping separation of old and new in trading—and there were no guilds.
The Jew could sell any kind of clothes, could produce them
or buy them secondhand or acquire them by bartering other
clothes. Whole phases of the development of the European
clothing trade of the Jews, handed down to us mainly by
hostile denunciations of the Christian tailor guilds fell away
in America where the Jew could start at once with what in
Europe had been developed only in the course of time. In
the invasion of the clothing industry, the Jew represented
the European element; Californian descriptions stress it as
an unfavorable feature of the Jew that his European clothes
were different from those of the other pioneers. But this
was only an expression of the fact that the Jew sold European clothing. As soon as a settlement was established, a
Jewish clothing store in the old style appeared.

That in trading clothes all human habits, prejudices, and
observations could easily appear is to be explained by the
understanding of the social importance of clothes "which
make people." Even before the Jew was the object of the

clothing joke, the tailor himself as the handyman of a social structure expressed by apparel, was the target of derision in all languages. The meaning of the English proverb, "Tailor . . . The ninth part of a man I think they call him"[40] had already appeared in America at the beginning of the nineteenth century, at a time when large parts of the American population still produced their clothes in their own households. Actually, therefore, a big leap was taken in the American popular consciousness from a state where clothes meant the personal needlework of the tailor to a situation where a whole new immigrant group, the German Jew, created a new sphere of activities of all kinds to produce them and trade in them. Even Shylock we find in the service of the so-necessary explanation of the clothing wonder. He transfers himself from the Rialto to Chatham Street and is busy with the so-necessary charity work of clothing nude, wild tribes.[41]

As soon as the Jew is symbolized by his role in the clothing trade, special features of that trade stand for him, also elsewhere, anywhere. In the same way features from entirely different economic spheres may be implanted into the clothing trade, if only these features are thought to be characteristic of the Jew.

The scattering of German-language particles strewn into the jokes of this period is as familiar to us as a light, marking off the German Jewish milieu. It remained even at a time when the achievement of the Jew in building up a clothing industry in America was already acknowledged and the Jewish business establishment no longer stood in the center of joke-smithing. It was then supplanted by the Jew's struggle to find a place in the social sphere with his neighbors, and the defeat he suffered in this field through his money philosophy and business habits, becomes the inheritor of the old joke system.

Clothing trade and pawnbroking aside, the stigma of Jewishness can stick to other less important businesses, although this connection is mostly only in passing. Such stigmas usually anticipate the expected comical effect, as for instance, when the derivative of the secondhand clothing trade, the lending of costumes for masked balls is concerned. In other cases the Jew is discredited as a dealer in works of art: His want of judgment in matters of art is pointed out by caricatures whose title line "Cut rates" tells us that even in the higher emanations of the human spirit the Jew can see only commodities. "The old masters—and how they are put on the market" set to work anew the ancient theme of the abyss between creation and marketing. Not satisfied with taking the already created work of art for marketing, the Jew may also initiate the creative process by importing the artist himself, and making him active in his business establishment. The artist may paint vases in the store window—an idea which, appropriately, would occur only to a merchant, "A. Bloomenfeld, dealer in Japanese goods," and stands also in refreshing contrast to old-fashioned methods of art instruction in art institutes.[42]

All in all, however, these characteristics of less obtrusive economic endeavors deemed to be Jewish, go out of fashion relatively quickly. A process of amalgamation is under way foreshadowing the idea that the Jew gives a peculiar shade to any undertaking, be it to an economic sector as a whole or only in a single business deal. It is called forth by his Jewishness, and by his acting according to principles that may be expected from him as a Jew. Now, here it is the general principles of business and typical reactions in all kinds of deals for which the Jew has to stand, in fact, it is the entire capitalistic course of business which is caricatured in him. There may have remained remembrances of the special occupations of the Jews of old, but they are felt more as remainders vis-à-vis the general development of the economic system. Thus, the clothing trade is no longer the only visible sign of their economic rise.

In addition to the general clothing scene the appendages of the store are drawn into the humoristic circle, viz: model dummies, advertising, and the display window. All these things meet us later in a meaning shifted to the role of the Jew in American society. Occasionally, by means of descriptions of the store, a legal problem of the business establishment may be mocked, too. In the caricature "How Hosenthal avoided a suit for damages," a business sign contains the ambiguous words, "Look out for our fall opening."[43]

Of those who saw the Jewish store owner in life and wanted to draw a realistic picture of him there were many. There were others who told anecdotes about him. In addition, there still existed a number of persons who could tell special stories about the other side of the coin, the mastering of the Jew by a real or assumed customer. The simple story unadorned by special effects, gives us only the description of a typical locality of many such stores, existing side by side, as a Chatham Street; a symbolic meaning not having yet been assigned to the whole:

> The air smelt of old coats and hats, and the side ways were glutted with dresses and over-coats and little, fat greasy children. There were country-men moving up and down the street, horribly harrassed and perplexed, and every now and then falling into the hands of one of these fierce-whiskered Jews, carried into a gloomy cavern, and presently sent forth again in a garment, coat or hat or breeches, in which he might dance, and turn his partner to boot. (1844).[44]

However, the passive role of the buyer in these descriptions ends with the appearance of robust natures on localities where such types could be expected as for instance on the levee in New Orleans:

> Debbils! says Tom; did ye never see sich a feller! Ax me if I take a hat, and when I say yes, and take der hat, and say "T'ankee" he jump 'pon me an' want his dollar an' 'half.[45]

In other cases cruelty may be an element of the situation itself, for instance in the Civil War story in which the sutler, an "old Jew" loses his money by the sudden marching off of the regiment:

> "Dare goes dat regiment out! Dey always fight like every ting. Dey git killed *effery von!* Who pays me my monish?"[46]

In spite of any incidents and accidents the store owner's daily life and philosophical mood, as we know it already from the pawnbroker, is accessible to a reader and in any case worth perpetuating through a diary. In the following "Israelite's Diary" we find such philosophical deliberations, the more remarkable because time and place (California of 1851) lead us to expect a much more restless diurnal life for a merchant there:

> I sweeps out de shope very soon. . . . Look out toors up street, town street, put sees nopody dat vants to puy close. Stand in toor two hours look at mans go py. . . . Von . . . trunk man vant dat fine blue preeches dat hange in de toor, wort von ounce [of gold dust]. I vas very bolite, and reques him to dry dem on. Ven he dry dem on he says he got no monish, and vants me to trost. He bromise to bay to-morrow, put I tells him very much I no trost, and he bulls off de breeches and goes away. . . . Von man goes py mit very old preeches mit de shirt tail out. I vas very bolite, and tells him I would make him very good close pargain; put he was broud, and says he no trades mit de Juice. . . . One of Crant's newsbaber poys dries to sell me a baber, but I shakes my head. De poy says very much old close, feefty tousand poxes, arrived in San Francisco, and 1.400 more Juice. Pad boy! . . . Valks up and town de shope and whistle till very late and dis vay I frightens de rats from eating de close.[47]

And as a precursor of the "glass put in" story on the New York east side we read further in the diary:

I studies to day how to make some monish py triving nails
a little biece into de poxes and bosts along de side valks,
vere mans could tear deir close.

In another story, the store is dominated by the restlessness
of its owner who, under the legal circumstances, shows "A
commercial paradox." The explanation of this caricature
is this:

> Customer: Say, Rothstein, who's that man doing all that
> yelling and screaming and swearing at the clerks in the
> rear of the store?
> Rothstein: Oh, dot vos Rosenberg, der silent pardner.[48]

c. *Summit Street (Broadway)*

If limitations force a man to walk in finite spaces, then
it certainly pays to choose what is assumed to be the longest
street in the world, Broadway, as the symbol of the stormy
forward impetus of the Jew; simply to show, by means of
humor and sarcasm, how the Jew "goes uptown" on Broadway in his business life and, consequently, also in his private
residence. In the first stages of this development, the economic success of the new immigrant class may still be in
doubt:

A good location.

Isaacheimer: How is dot cousin of yours gettin' along?
Cohenstein: Pretty good. He vas doin' buziness on
Broadway.
Isaacheimer: On Broadway? And he's only six months in
der country! Vot line is he in?
Cohenstein: Matches, shoe laces undt suspenders.[49]

Where all buildings are overcrowded with business
establishments, the newly arrived immigrant can only find
a place for himself with new ideas. The caricature "A coming business innovation" shows us Broadway, blocked with

the boxes of the intruder, containing merchandise, and lets us hear the basic idea of this innovation:

> Vot's der use paying rent? Der sidewalk is free! Vait till dem oder Broadway merchants haf by dot idea tumbled— all der stores will be empty, alretty![50]

All at once, as fast as only the transition from good to bad can be, all of Broadway is at stake. Of course, the later historian sees it in another light; he can detect the signs of the time which predicted the coming flood, and accompanies "Lowenstein and Frisman" with the statement that it was the first Jewish sign to appear on Broadway and that they thought, in the course of the next forty years, there might be one sign on Broadway which would not be Jewish.[51]

Full use was made of such prophecies, the humor of later times revolving exclusively around the question as to what to do with the last remaining Gentile business sign left. One suggested solution was to sell a look at the sign through a spyglass: "Last chance 10¢ a peep." An opposite solution undertakes to take down the sign forever and, by means of a caricature, to perpetuate the view of the Jews assembled to celebrate the event. In the first version we see Broadway overflowing with business signs of Jewish firms. A large number of people are lined up, in the form of a dollar sign, to pay for a peep at the Gentile sign which, to be sure, is already hanging on the last floor, the title of the firm "George Jones" drawn in small letters; whereas the Jewish firm names "Goldberg and Silverstein," "Cohenstein *und* Co.," "Rosenstein," "Finkelstein und Co.," "Blumenstein," "Lowenstein," "Oppenheim," "Schonheimer Bros." appear glamorously, in big shining letters. The cartoon offers this as final proof that the "—heimers" and "—steiners," now firmly entrenched on Broadway, will finally also socially go "uptown." A novum is offered by a red advertising sign "Semiannual Firesale" and, as a subtle intimation, we see another sign bearing the name "Morris Burnheimer."

A further solution shows us:

The Dream of the Jews realized.

Ceremony of taking down the last sign of the Christians
in New Jerusalem (Formerly New York).[52]

The sign "John Smith and Co." is taken down and
another, "Moses Eichstein Son a. Levy" is put up. In the
jubilant mob of Jews having come to view this spectacle,
naturally the "Pawnbrokers'" Union is prominent. "Chakey
Einstein, owff Broadway" then becomes representative of the
successful Jewish merchant who goes uptown. We shall have
to follow his much more protracted and, in so many respects,
frustrated rise to the heights of American "Society." The
Broadway glory is the only thing all those Jews are permitted
to possess without any challenge:

> Myriad signs along the street
> Israelitish names repeat. . . .
> Surely you're on to day,
> Chakey Einstein, owff Broadway.[53]

CHAPTER 6

The New Society

THE ENTRANCE of the Jew into the new society in America comes about at a time when the country is undergoing great economic changes. To be sure, this represents a sharp contrast to Europe where the Jew enters the capitalistic economy and society without too drastic a change in his economic functions. Although, therefore, the social criticism of American humor stigmatizes mainly the new position of the Jew in the American world, there are nevertheless some old European stereotypes rigidified into folklore that lived on in America. They, too, are strong enough to keep the humorist busy. One wonders about the strength of the medieval *Judenschwein*[1] when one sees it dealt with in free creations through the American humorist. However, the old atrocity of the theme vanished in many ways. As long as unified concepts of Jewish types were not reached, the swine and its consumption forbidden to the Jew, remained target and instrument of humor pointing out the Jew. The many uses of this folkloristic theme entered the most varied language media, puns, fantastic tales and so on.[2] Even in newer layers of humor we still find comparisons like: "I have detested the devil as a Jew hates a hog;"[3] the real impetus of

76

"A Jew de Spree" (*Life*, Vol. 14, 1889, p. 299).

the theme, however, is again diverted to social criticism, this time, however, in several directions. A rich opportunity for this kind of humor is given by the swine plague of American cities, first in New York, so often described in American literature:

> . . . we were frequently turned upon by those ferocious brutes, who imbued me, during my short sojourn in their neighborhood, with a perfectly Jewish antipathy to the whole swinish multitude.[4]

With Jewish social types definitely established, New York's plague may be illuminated by a humoristic protest of an imagined speaker for the Jews:

Pigs.

Mrs. Grundy:

Hath not a Jew eyes? Hath not a Jew a nose? Are not Jews the most orderly and the most musical among our tax-paying inhabitants? Why, then, must their eyes and olfactories be so constantly offended, and their ears excruciated, by the passage of endless droves of the "Abominable Beast" through the streets? Have you not read the Bible, Madam? and do you not know that swine are "Unclean" animals in our sight?

I am a well-to-do Child of Israel, and reside, with my family, in a spacious house in an up-town street near the Fifth Avenue. We are lovers of music and—especially during the summer months—partial to fresh air. By my desire, my children practice Music several hours a day; but are always forced to do so with closed windows, except on the first day of the week (when, to conciliate our neighbours prejudices, I abstain from business, and am enabled to accompany my daughter on the violoncello). On that day my parlor windows are opened, for on that day alone are we safe from the abomination of our race. At all other times my shutters are permanently closed, and a watch is stationed on the upper floors to give timely notice of the nauseous advent. On they come by hundreds, big and little, fat and lean, heralded by cracking of whip lashes and shouts of men; grunting, squealing, emitting a most pungent odor; some in wagons, unable from obesity to walk; others scattering upon the sidewalks, running hither and thither, pursued by men and boys; and creating such a scene of confusion as could not have been paralleled by the herd possessed of devils.

If these things must be, can they not be reserved for Christian eyes and noses? Must we, nearly every day of the week, undergo processes of purification from involuntary contamination? Is it fair that we, who swell so considerably the wealth and numbers of the land, should be at the mercy of the Pork-driving rabble? Is there no exclusively Christian district through which a route may be prescribed for these sources of fleas and all manner of uncleanliness? or, rather cannot immunity from the nuisance be guaranteed to some one or two streets, wherein our people may find a home? Pray, Madam, influence the *City-Fathers* to look with pitying eyes upon our sufferings. Induce them to forget for once the nationality of naturalization; to remove the styes upon the city's sight in Shanty Town, and to legislate against the *swinish* multitude.

Respectfully yours
Judäus Apelles.[5]

Nevertheless, occasionally a comic story may still be invented in which the Jew in America, too, is tortured by his fellowmen on this point. Such a tale is purposefully placed at a far distance, where it gains in color as a curiosity and because the occurrence took place on a voyage:

San Francisco, June 10th, 1853.

The sympathies of the community have been strongly excited within the last few days in favor of an unfortunate gentleman of the Hebrew persuasion, on whom the officers of the Golden Gate perpetrated a most inhuman atrocity, during her late trip from Panama. I gather from information of indignant passengers, and by contemplation of an affecting appeal to the public, posted in the form of a handbill at the corners of the streets, that this gentleman was forced, by threats and entreaties, to do violence to his feelings and constitution, by eating his way through a barrel (not a half barrel, as had been stated by interested individuals, anxious to palliate the atrocious deed), of clear pork! The handbill alluded to is headed by a graphic and well executed sketch by Solomon ben David, a distinguished artist of this city. . . .[6]

A new literary version of the pork hater is the anecdotal transgression of the ritual food prohibition in the way it occurs in the conscience of the Jew:

> . . . A German Jew . . . eating a pork-chop in a thunderstorm. On hearing an unusually loud clap, he laid down his knife and fork, and observed, "Vell, did any poty efer hear such a fuss apout a little pid o' bork!"[7]

Naturally, the summit of American swine humor is reached in no other way than through a bet, the losing Gentile appears in it as a fellow without humor:

> The prisoner, seeing the Jew's eagerness to commence the feast, now began to repent his bargain, and considered that he had in some measure played the fool to give a person a shilling to eat up all his sausages, merely for the pleasure of seeing a Jew eat swine's flesh. . . .[8]

The deepest sounds of sarcasm, however, finds the humorist in the swine plague of the twentieth century, expressing itself in the stockyards investigation. Mr. Dooley has the following to say about it, directly from his Chicago residence:

> What ails me? . . . Haven't r-read about th' invistygation in th' Stock Yards? It's a good thing f'r ye ye haven't. If ye, knew what that ham—oh, th' horrid wurrud—was made iv ye'd go down to Rabbi Hirsch an' be baptized f'r a Jew.[9]

The theme of the baptized Jew, likewise reduced to folklore, appears in American literary humor. It is used mostly as a critical yardstick to measure effectiveness of the activities of the conversionist societies. Unsuccessful endeavors of the Jewish mission are laughed off as a deception of the Christian public and as a folly of queer people. As an exception, this time it is not the Jew who pays the bill but his comic would-be missionary. We see this best in a story which allows us, also, a practical inside view into the "business" of the conversionist societies and reveals the methods of their money-collections. The salaried missionary appears as the only beneficiary of these benign institutions:

American Society for Ameliorating the Condition of the Jews.

The Society met last evening. Notwithstanding the tremendous thunderstorm, and torrents of rain, four old ladies with three umbrellas made their appearance; we forgot the Rev. *Dr. Dumwho* came in a cab, at the expense of the Society. The Rev. Dr. having chosen his text, commenced by reminding them of the miserable condition of the Jews, their want of knowledge, their impossibility to get along in the next world, as well as they did in this; spoke of the holy purpose of the Society—of himself individually—of the three old ladies in particular (upon this the three old ladies sniffled and looked extremely meek and pious) and ended with an earnest appeal for more funds. Hereupon the plate was handed round. *John Donkey* having crept in from the rain, modestly rose up, and spoke of the distress at home, mentioned many families in his neighborhood, who were wanting the necessaries of life, remarked the advantage of ameliorating the conditions of the Five Points, and wound up with a desire that the funds be devoted for their particular brethren, whose condition, both morally and physically, demanded more attention than the Jews.

Upon this an evident uproar was heard. One old lady, sternly called him "an atheist"—another indulged in some slight doubts where he might go to when he died—the third, words being wanting, sternly shook her umbrella at him, and the Rev. Dr. concluded by calling him "an ass," at which *John Donkey* walked out, determined to keep fast his sixpence.

After this the subscription was taken up, each old lady pulling forth a quarter, and dropping it exactly on its edge, so as to make it ring distinctly—then went home happy with the idea of having saved a nation from hell and the devel.

Proceeds of the evening fund	D. cts.
for emelioring the conditions of the Jews	25
	25
	25
	—
	75
cab for Rev. Dr. Dum, going and coming in rain D	1.00
	75
	—
balance in favor of Dr. D.	25[10]

The results, wholly inadequate when compared with the money sacrifice made, are further derided in pointing out the inferiority of the baptized subject and his shrewdness in causing more and more expenses to be wasted upon him. At the same time, it is also disclosed that the missionary machinery, once created, moves according to its own laws, has its own need to advertise, and acts solely in harmony with these needs, not in following the basic idea of mission:

The Society for Ameliorating the Condition of the Jews, having at an incalculable expense at last obtained "A Real live reformed Jew, Moses Aaron Meshumet," take great pleasure in exhibiting this unique animal to the Christian Public.

He is young and of an engaging disposition, at the same time extremely shrewd.

He will for the amusement of the audience, state how and when, and for what consideration, he became a convert,—read chapters from the Testament forwards and backwards.—together with many other interesting feats.

The whole to conclude by his eating a pound of pork-sausages and a real ham.

Admittance 12½ cents. Front seats for the ladies.[11]

Also the Jew deserting Judaism, but not accepting Christi-
anity, leaving a vacuum, was derided:

It was said of a crafty Israelite, who deserted the Hebrew
faith without embracing that of the Christians, and yet
endeavoured to make both Parties subservient to his own
selfish views, that he resembled the blank leaf between the
Old and New Testament, belonging to neither, and making a cover of both.[12]

a. *The social face of the Jew*

To make use of the physical visibility of his victim is the
strong side of humor and, where the Jew carries these physical
features "nosology" is in place:

The English nose is apt to be thick and cartilaginious;
that of the Jew somewhat crooked.[13]

However, where on a higher plane the mental visage of
the Jew is to be formed on the ground of social features, his
physical appearance becomes no longer useful for the humorist. He then discovers the Jew if he finds his imagined
qualities or is reminded of him where such qualities are
found also in other people. Social reaction to this becomes
the inevitable:

Lynching.

. . . We quote from the Boston *Gazette* of March 31, 1776,
a file of which is before us.
We hear that a person in a neighboring government lately
refused to pay a debt for which he was attached, because
the writ was not stamped; the populace immediately upon
hearing thereof, assembled, and having the fellow before
them, passed the three following votes and resolves, viz:
Vote 1. That this man is not a Christian.
Vote 2. That he ought to be of some religion.
Therefore 3dly, voted That he be a Jew.
Whereupon, Resolved, That, he be circumcized.
This resolution so terrified the poor creature, that he
begged forgiveness for his impudence, and promised to

behave better for the future, he was then permitted to make a Confession of Faith; Upon which the sentence was remitted and he dismissed.[14]

In this case the spiritual Judaizer is branded by the most visible peculiarity of the Jew, circumcision. He is appointed a "circumcized Christian" in the sense of the Christian polemical literature of old. However, the more intimate features of the Jewish face in humor are all built on the imagined intimate habits of the Jew and, therefore, demand a more complicated answer. Money, sentiment, and fighting for the principles of money stand here on the topmost line; also as a factor of social visibility it is to be noted well:

You are a Jew.

"You are a Jew," said one man to another: "when I bought this from you, it was to be a Guinea, and now you demand five-and-twenty shillings, which is more than you asked." "For that very reason," replied the other, "I am no Jew, for a Jew always takes less than he asks."[15]

The hunt for signs of hidden Judaism is symbolized through the many puns with the word, "Jew." Because, if simply everything from the Jewish milieu can be brought to comic effect, a mere verbal error echoing the sound of "Jew" may already cause laughter. Conscious of this possibility, the inventors of these puns are tireless in fabricating new Jewish word relations and we shall find later the caricaturists just as untiring in their hunt after new possibilities:

Jewing and Chewing

—Nothing can be more obvious, than, that those *elegantees* and literary *prodiges,* who pronounce the d like j, and t like ch, on the Authority of Walker, (who, by the way, neither teaches nor justifies it), are sound and sagacious critics. Only consider, that *due* and *dues* should be pronounced *Jew* and *Jews* and you at once have the *origin* of the Jews and the term "Jewing." *That* people's love of pelve is proverbial; and their art and perseverance in getting others in debt, or having great sums *due* from them, and making money by *sharp* dealing, very naturally gives that process the name of *Jewing,* and the Practiser that of *Jew.* Hence, too, a Jewsharp, that is a Jew-sharp. Hence, it is, moreover, that when a clever Irishman wishes to have a fight, or *duel,* with a countryman, he says, "my *jewel!* and knocks him down, at the *first* bid, as the auctioneers call it—or by way of earnest (as the lawyers term it), or *pay down,* to take the case out of a Statute of frauds."[16]

But the public, in general, is not in need of such phonetic finesses or far-fetched puns. To it, types of life are represented which give rise to a picture of a Jewish society dependent solely upon the retort of imagination.

b. *Jewish Society: Status and Intercourse.*

In considering the problem "Israel among the nations," there is a turning point at the moment economic relations proceed towards social intercourse. Thus, the economic functions of the Jews in a country were, at all times, more or less clear in contemporary opinion or even in the crooked mirror of the wit of the time. We move, however, to new psychological territory where the Jew, by his social intercourse with the Gentile should be a co-laborer in developing the general society. In that stage of social development, the New World, in which the latecomer meets an already secluded social class of earlier arrivals, is naturally different from Europe, where existed the contemporaneity of all social layers, Gentile and Jew, as a historical fact for many centuries. In the New World, however, a class of new immigrants had to fight for social recognition and the place allocated to them was, in great part, a consequence of their economic success. To be sure, there were limits to this, and Jewish wealth, or other achievement, could not leap over a social barrier wherever the new caste in America had built a wall for the explicit purpose of keeping at a distance the well-to-do of a new immigrant class.

In the new country it is sociability, the ability to become impressed by the facts of society life, that means everything. Naturally, there must be rules of exclusion; without a circle of people forced to remain outside, "good" society is not possible. In the New World at least two generations make the gentleman, and this rule was sufficient to keep out all otherwise successful German Jewish people. It is always pointed out as a fact that August Belmont was the only Jew admitted to exclusive social intercourse and that this exception was a consequence of his being married to a Gentile. Jewish exclusion remained the normal situation. Thus the subterranean activity of the excluded to set aside the barrier, at least in individual cases, was the more eager. That such an activity opened the door to wit and humor as the mirror of frustrated endeavors is easily understandable. The fight for unimpeded social intercourse is substituted for the struggle to achieve economic success as a basic theme of wit.

Matters of status precede the question of social intercourse. A Jew has to have status in his own society and Jewish society as a whole has to reach status first in the eyes of Gentiles. Then the Jew has to put up a request for admission to social relations with the Gentile. Both basic problems were spotted at once by the sharp eye of the humorist and his creations in words and drawings mock both things, the notion of status in Jewish society and the strife for social intercourse with the Gentiles.

The theme of the nobility of the ancient Jewish people constituting the status of the Jew even in a later world, comes first. The attempt of the Jew to maintain this status is shown as an unsuccessful rebellion against the fences of "good" society. If only for that reason, the status claim of the Jew further propelled by imitation of high society life, is ironically mocked:

At the fancy-dress ball.

Mr. Minzesheimer: Vell, Mrs. Chones, How you like dot ancestral gostume of mine?
Mrs. Jones: Ancestral Mr. Minzesheimer? Why, it's a Rubens costume!
Mr. Minzesheimer: Dot's all right. Dot's my tribe. Ruben, Simon, Levi, Dan—all dem fellers was my ancestors, don't it?[17]

His subconscious ancestor-cult was, in this way, derided as a product of his ignorance—Rubens was not known to him; more direct fun at the expense of his forefathers is also not missing:

What Jewish Tribe would make the best sheriff officers?— The *Levy* tribe.[18]

All searches for tribes, lost or found, could, therefore, not secure the Jew.

Furthermore, noblesse oblige and patronizing the arts as the ticket for entry into "good" society is likewise mocked at; the artist cannot detect anything other than money interest in this, either.

Defending his work.

Mrs. Isaacstein: Do you t'ink you haf caught eggsactly Meester Isaacstein's eggspression?
The Sculptor: Oh, surely, Madam!
Is not dot a fine eggspression?—vun mighd say a pluto-gratic eggspression![19]

That the Jew is not "clubbable" in the sense of the Gentile club, is shown by his concept of his own clubs. In the caricature "At the Isra-Elite Club" Mr. Dinkelspiel's savings in inviting his friend Mr. Ickstein from St. Louis as a guest to his club, are described.[20]

In his claim to social intercourse with the Gentile, the European *entrée billet,* baptism, is not acknowledged. Bap-

AT THE FANCY-DRESS BALL.

MR. MINZESHEIMER.—Vell, Mrs. Chones, how you like dot aencestral gostume off mine?

MRS. JONES.—Ancestral, Mr. Minzesheimer? Why, it's a Rubens costume!

MR. MINZESHEIMER.—Dot's all right. Dot's my tribe. Reuben, Simeon, Levi, Dan—all dem was my aencestors, don't it?

At the fancy dress ball *(Puck,* Vol. 14, 1883/84, p. 391).

tism of the Jew doesn't contribute anything essential to the degrees of social life in America. There is nothing changed by it in appearance and air. The Jew insisting on his certificate of baptism, becomes ridiculous. In a caricature portraying a Jewish family refused admission to a Staten Island inn, their attempt to legalize their position for admission by a previous baptism is especially derided:

"A hopeless case—with Apologies to Mr. E. Fawcett."

Oh, gaily they marched, that Hebrew crowd
To the inn from which Jews were excluded:
. . . And the father marched up to the clerk as proud
As ever a millionaire Jew did.
. . . For that clerk he said: "You're an Hebrew Jew,
And you cannot put up at *this* inn!"
And Herr Meyer answered:
"And my family *vas got christen!*"
But the clerk inspected them all, and his head
Most dubiously was shaken:
"You *may* have been just baptized," he said:
"But it doesn't seem to have taken."[21]

In vain also is his solicitude for the well-being of the Gentile society. In the following anecdote the ridicule of such a notion is further heightened by the manner in which the Jew undertakes to show his patriotic impulse by his own money loss:

A certain Jew who had lost money in the Kean failure was loudly bewailing his loss to me last Friday. As a sort of Job's comfort I said: "Oh, well! Others are in the same boat!" "Oxkoose me," he replied. "I em nod dinking oaf der monish; but vat a horrubule blow der vailure ish do Medidiseems . . .[22]

Competition among gentlemen is the true meaning of the American Sporting Scene and the sport bet of the onlookers represents free valuation of coming events through gentlemen, in accord with society rules. As soon as the Jew—even only in Gentile imagination—appears on the sporting scene, he enters, in the opinion of the Gentiles, into an inadmissible competition, the competition with Gentiles on the social field. To his bet, likewise, the same defect adheres; he thinks only in business ways and is therefore unfit for evaluation of sports events which have to be based on personal experience in having taken part in sport:

> For no Jew, in Time's long course
> Ever backed a winning horse . . .[23]

The field on which a man can prove his value, the golf course, is the gentlemen's sport *kat exochen* and the confusion of the Jew at his first sport trial appears with his first hit:

At the links.

"Vell, Isaacs vos not so good a golf blayer as he vos a peezness man."
"You bet not! He don't foozle much in his peezness!"[24]

As the summit of the rejection of the Jew outdoors or vacationing, inexhaustible in its humoristic exploitation, stands his rejection from hotel and summer resort. In this field, wit always gains a new reality by the push of hostile forces renewing their activities from year to year. Actually, one incident replaced the other and the periodical publishing of humoristic literature became the more facile through a seasonal issue which could be counted on with certainty. The preliminary discussions, where the Jew has to go for his summer vacation, was followed by the first humorous reports on incidents in hotels and spas. The Jew was dragged through every imaginable situation by the humorous journals during the summer months, when the contact of a paper of this kind with its readers tends to weaken. Love and gratefulness for a theme which represents a first prize, flows from all these drawings of beach scenes, the indecent exposure in the undressing of Jewish bodies, and the never aging bon mots. The preview of the press on the coming Jewish "season" is reported in this way:

It is now the season for a *Herald* reporter to interview the proprietors of leading Summer Hotels, and to elicit the information that only white Jews will be welcome in their establishments.[25]

The main feature of the theme of the humor of the rejected Jew is his endeavor to fight for his putative right to be admitted. In consequence, if his arguments and open efforts do him no good, the humorist exults in demonstrating the Jew's ingenuity in inventing technical devices and psychological disguises whose purpose was to put an end to his misfortunes.

First, he is shown as ridiculous if he believes himself to be in a position to presume on his rights:

Unfair discrimination.

. . . Weil I am an American citizen, Ich habe mein rights, and I vants to board vere I likes.
Ikey Moses, Old Clo'.
P.S. "I encloses mein bizziness card."[26]

The next illusion, that by undergoing baptism a Jew may become the exception to the social rules, is just as easily destroyed.[27] Having exhausted these possibilities, America's wonders of technical science only then rise before our eyes. "Hints for the Jews—Several ways of getting to Manhattan Beach"[28] shows us a balloon flying over the beach and letting Jews down softly to land on it. The "War against the Jews"[29] is the ultimate among the hostile titles of these caricatures. In a further "hint to the Hebrews. How they make themselves independent of the watering place hotels,"[30] a skyscraper is built on a bathing platform and inhabited up to the last floor by Jews.

Not neglected, the psychological approach is also not held in contempt and, in truth, proves at times to be fruitful:

Bound to be in it.

Lippheimer: How you got in dot hotel, Meyer? I understood dey don't take none of our people.
Meyer: Sh-h-h—I vas a Brahmin—Maya Baba Schunda Sen—it vas a good racket—only I can't eat no meat![31]

The main rounds in the battle of the Jews against restrictive policies, as in the Seligman incident in Saratoga (1877) and, later, the closing of Manhattan Beach, have made their mark in American social history. These occurrences naturally found themselves mirrored in contemporary humor because they were widely discussed in the daily press. As a Cause, the Saratoga incident also called forth, on the part of caricaturists a more serious attitude, as that of "Puck" against Hilton,[32] whereas the later Manhattan Beach case was felt mostly as an incitement to humor. It was exploited in never-ending humoristic explosions, whereby the connection with Saratoga was kept fresh:

Corbin's Boomerang.

. . . But the cheek of Corbin! He is playing himself as a tail on Judge Hilton's kite; and he wants to be bigger than the kite itself. Hilton was content with closing his tavern against the children of Israel: but Mr. Corbin desires to close the gates of his railway, his hotel, his Jew music-blower and the free Atlantic Ocean to the Jews. . . .[33]

Headlines illuminate the conflict: "War against Jewry," and hilarious telegrams are received from the "battleground:" Manhattan Beach for the "clo' religionists of the Rothschilds."[34] The humorist is also prepared to indulge in a bit of heroics, and maudlin self-pity:

Puck's Picnic.

. . . He did not go to Manhattan Beach, for Puck counts a Jew or two among his intimate acquaintances. . . .[35]

PUCK'S PICNIC.—PUCK AND HIS CONTRIBUTORS BY THE SEA.

Puck's picnic *(Puck*, Vol. 5, 1879, pps. 345-46).

Finally, as a climax to the text, he shows us his own "Picnic" at Manhattan Beach; politicians dressed in bathing suits in the water and, the only Jew admitted among them, "A. Belmont."[36]

Time is given to explore the situation in a realistic way with humorous endings. For instance, an interview of a journalist investigating the matter with an owner of a summer hotel excluding Jews is reported in this way:

No Jews admitted?

This will be a Christian Colony! Said Mr. Hughes. "Jews, of course you consider highly objectionable characters?" the reporter continued, with the rising inflection.
"They are not Christians, certainly. Of course, I am not illiberal in these matters. . . . But of course, my colony is a Christian colony. . . ."[37]

However, the humorist has but to make a half-turn and the Jew is demonstrated as a snob toward his own people, refusing their company:

Mr. Mitzenheimer in search of a Hotel.

". . . Oh, no! we have nothing but Jews here. No Gentiles allowed on the premises."
"Den I don't stay here uf you pay me fifty dollars a day. You reckon respectable Chews goin' to bee coobed up off do demselves like day vas some inferior animals."[38]

c. *Jewish Society: Status and the Social Life.*

The barrier to the "good" society of the Gentiles erected, the Jew remained within his own society and, in illuminating this society, the humorist gives free rein to his imagination. What place the Jew takes in his own society and with whom he intermingles there, is entirely dependent on the humorist's notion of this society, and he never tires of showing what he thinks of it. At this point, he leaves the ground of common American experience for the first time preferring to display an illusion of another, unreal, American society that, thank goodness, looks better than the real one. This imagined society can, therefore, feel better if it can look down on Jewish society.

Before the humorist can get to work, Jewish society must first be tainted. The physical appearance of the Jew now must stand for Jewish society, and something like an aura must surround everything Jewish, differentiating it from the "good" Gentile society and making the difference accessible to the senses. Thus, caricaturing the social life of the Jew begins with his behavior. Only later will he—the caricaturist —elaborate on this, artfully, in all its facets; indeed, the early handling of the theme deals with the exterior impression called forth by the Jew's physical features; His appearance is displayed, correctly, and roaring laughter is assured to all those who are dedicated to a belief in this appearance. If the cruelty of caricature generally catches the totally visible, without any true relationship to the inner man, so it is also in the case of the Jew where there is, at work, in addition, the already long accepted notion of his appearance which existed in people who had never seen a Jew in their private lives. It is the nose-motif, stressing the extraordinary size of the scenting organ of the Jew, that overwhelms the audience in humoristic drawings and texts. There is no need for any textual explanation if, further, in purely caricaturistic facial studies, "His special features,"[39] on one side of the special treatment vouchsafed the nose, the eyebrows are drawn in the form of the dollar sign. The caricature may be given a direct title, "Noses,"[40] or be embellished with a more ornamental language like "Types of Humanity (mostly from "foreign foundries") formed in the fields;"[41] it never fails to work with full accuracy of aim, because it is always sure of what it means.

In this corporeal aspect, the Jew has his effect even if he exists proportionately in the weakest dilution, even if he is the last Jew:

Of the Jews, there was but *one,* and that *one* was supposed to be the last of the lost tribe! He certainly had that appearance.[42]

In more serious literary elaborations, too, the notion of the extraordinary quality of the Jewish nose, designating its owner as a Jew, is present. According to an opinion of a traveler the attribute of snoring corresponds with it, against which a Yankee cure would well be in place:

The man who slept in the berth next mine snored frightfully. . . . Evidently, he was a German Jew, and his nose, acoustically considered, seemed well adapted for the involuntary transmission of vast volumes of sound. An ingenious Yankee has patented a cure for snoring which all snorers ought to purchase previous to night-travelling.[43]

In a use shifted to self-comparison, "like the wandering Jew," a historical image may even be revealed: man walks after his nose like the Israelites after the Biblical pillar of fire:

Our march resembled very much that uv the children uv Israel. Our noses wuz the pillers uv fire by nite, and our breath the pillar uv smoke by day.[44]

From the Jewish viewpoint, "seen through Synagoggles,"[45] the thing is not entirely funny. It is the humorist's special delight to imagine the panic called forth in the Jews by being forced to look at their own faces through the mirror of caricature. Here, also, the lackadaisical reaction of the Jew, compared with the attitude of other objects of American caricature, is especially mocked:

How you laugh, Levi, when they display an American with big ears. . . . But you say it is a shame to pick out any particular race when Mr. Moses Isaacs Levi is portrayed with a Jumbo nose. . . . Ah, Levi, the one trouble is that we are

> not hard-headed Saxons and Teutons, nor witty minded
> Latins, but Levi, we are Asiatics. Levi, we are not Euro-
> peans, nor Americans. . . . How glad a Christian is to say,
> "He's a white Jew."—meaning that he is an elegant man
> in his essential character. . . .[46]

The interpretation of the expression, "white Jew" is telling
vis-à-vis earlier and later uses of the phrase in Europe. As
used in the new German language, its meaning is exactly the
contrary of its later usage: a German of Jewish sentiment,
user of Jewish maxims of behavior. But an imported article
sometimes changes its trademark even in the field of ideas.

Aside from the visual appearance of the Jew, there is, above
all, the aura, invisible as air, and fully loaded with the voltage
that forces one to be aware of the presence of the Jew, an
awareness not created by any outspoken situations caused by
his behavior. Such hints are made visible in the innumerable
puns, often maintained in artificial word convulsions, intimations of the "Jew" appearing in all possible lingual and verbal
formations and disfigurements. In full strength this might
be supported by the outcry:

Y is the Yew that made them all squack![47]

Corresponding to the puns, is the manner of spelling a
word so that, often, the mere spelling gives an intimation of
a situation with a Jew therein. "I am no jewty," sez I[48] may
be placed in the mouth of a policeman. The gentleman of
the jury may be a "jewryman."[49] A certain application of
reason may be "jewdishus."[50] "The Juice"[51] as the title of a
Jewish story implies human qualities which have to do with
taste; this joking expression was already to be found in older
anecdotes.[52] Compared to a "jewell," the Jew exists already
in a riddle of one of the oldest of such collections (1830):

Puzzles.

Why is a Hebrew in a fever like a diamond?
Ans. Because he is a Jew ill (jewel)."[53]

The pun motif maintained itself for a long time, its frequent imitations becoming more and more tasteless and finally connected with old clothes:

> One of the principal dealers in "Old Clo," in New York, is named Weller, and is universally known among his friends as the Jew-Weller (Jeweller)."[54]

Occasionally the pun-motif is degraded to a level of pure idiocy, so that even icicles from the Jewish clothing store are called "Isaac-les."[55] However, all this is indispensable for the daily use of humorous journals, because the "air" around the Jew in society has to be produced without interruption, eventually even artificially pumped in.

A fine scenting nose can smell out this atmosphere even where it might not ordinarily be conjectured to exist:

> If she discovered the true inwardness of this Anglo-Saxon "Jews-desprit," she refrained from saying anything about it.[56]

But the crowning pun with which the Jew is crowned is the word play suggesting the Olympian, "Jewbither,"[57] in its use, likewise, quite old (1836). From the sublime of this name to the ridiculous of naming a dog is only a short leap—still containing some stories of human passion:

"Jew-Peter.

"Head-Centre of Olympus, a suspicious, speculating nervous God, very jealous of his wife,"[58] whereby passion may still be exchanged for something else, viz., another religion. The real meaning of this change is not entirely lost:

> Professor Crowell says that Rome in exchanging her religion exchanged Jupiter for *Jew* Peter. This is considered a remarkable pun.[59]

The series of Jewish dog-names usually do not go beyond the Judas complex; therefore, it must be regarded as an

advance if the quadruped gets the name of the chief Greek
god instead that of the traitor. However, such shining goal
could have sinister motives, too, as the following derisive
commentary shows:

> Sam Spillkins is the owner of a very fine dog, which
> accompanies him in his walks. He was passing Mose
> Schaumburg's store, on Austin Avenue, when Mose's
> attention was called to the dog.
> "Dot ish a shplendid dog, Mr. Spillkins. Vat is his name?"
> asked Mose.
> "His name is Peter. Yes, Peter."
> "Peter—dot ish a very shingular name, Mr. Spillkins."
> His real name, Mr. Schaumburg is Jupiter, but I always
> leave off the Jew part of Jupiter and call him Peter, on
> account of the high regard I have for Israelites as Ameri-
> can citizens. I don't like to use the word Jew in connection
> with the name of a dog. Come here, Peter. Do you see
> how he knows his name?"
> Mose beamed all over with joy, and made some pathetic
> remarks about how much better the Jews are treated in
> this country than in Russia, and Spillkins thinks he has
> laid the foundation for a trade for a fall overcoat on a
> credit basis.
>
> —Texas Sifting.[60]

In earlier centuries, people who gave their dogs Biblical
names were decried as atheists; the Olympian dog's name,
therefore, gives a double pleasure if the Jew gets his due.

Real heavenly joy, however, radiates from the musical
instrument bearing the Jew's name, and the "Jew's harp,"
by the mere mention of its name, raises joyous connotations
of all kinds associated with the Jews of old:

> Some have wondered how a celebrated Jew of antiquity
> could have plaid on his Jews harp and *sing at the same
> time*. But, as an old lady on the steamboat once remarked
> to me, "folks were smarter in those days than they are
> now."[61]

As early as 1831, the Jew's harp already spoke its own language of comparison with the Jews, as when it is said of Terpsichore: "And from her gentle Jews harp sprung The soft vibrations of the *Jewish tongue*."[62] Finally, the language of the Jew's harp became even more outspoken, so that the tone really made music:

> "Did you ever see a jews harp?" remarked Smith to Brown while looking in a store window the other day.—"No," rejoined Brown, "but I have frequently seen a Jew sharp."[63]

Such puns belong to the oldest inventory of American humor. *"Jew Nipper*. Spelt Juniper" can already be found in 1824 in an American book for juveniles.[64] The *"Jew-roar"* as one of the gentlemen of the jury, and the *"Jew-risdiction"* date from 1836;[65] "the *Yewnited Brethering*" came not much later.[66] How far poor pronunciation of English incited such vagaries of fantasy is to be seen from early linguistic admonitions:

> With some people a preceding *d* is softened by the iotized u into j; so that I heard one of these persons, who had prejudice against the Hebrew race, object to residence at a suburb of New York, where many of that thrifty people lived, and went daily to business in the city, remark with savage wit, that he found the place would not suit him, because of the depressing dampness—the morning and the evening Jews.[67]

Once humor exploited to the full all the imponderables in the setting of Jewish society, the demonstration of things occurring there may begin.

Heading all else, were the nostalgic recollections of those distant earlier stages of the "good" society before the Jews entered her golden (American) age. In addition, the Jew's love of sumptuousness, the whole character of his way of spending money came under fire. It was deemed a sheer love of luxury by the descendants of the Puritans, without an inner relationship to cultural goods, an overrating of all the externals of man. They felt in him a strangeness to the easy-going attitudes of the social atmosphere, a lack of tradition in all highly developed activities of "good" society, be it art or sport, love of nature or personal intercourse between men. His lack of an inner relationship to nature is a source of laughter in a scene in which he, to try the echo in the woods and knowing no other word, calls the name of a Jewish business associate, to which the confused echo answers with a second Jewish name:

Trying the Echo:

Hebraic Tourist: Dinkelspiel!
Echo (Confused): Minzheimer.[68]

A man who is found to be defective in the area of the enjoyment of nature, remains unfulfilled also when he returns to the drawing room. He is frustrated even if he tries to find his way back to nature from the drawing room by trying to master a sport, like golf, or the horses, in a select company. The corresponding pictures become a mirror of his frustrations. The unreachable distance of inherited art patronage and grasped drawing room activity can be seen from the American adaptation of one of the oldest Rothschild jokes. In Europe the "playing of two persons on one piano" stresses the ignorance of the Jewish provincial looking at Rothschild's palace interior. In the American version the bon mot characterizes the snobbish attitude of the Jew to his own society:

The Duett at the Goldstein Reception.

Ikenheimer: My, My Ain't dese hardt times awful! Dose Goldstein girls has both to blay off der same piano![69]

Especially illuminating are the intimations in relation to the cardplaying of the American Jews. From the viewpoint of cultural history, we must see in this activity, at least in part, a withdrawing to a harmless pastime in the intimacy of one's own home, and not in a public place, of people not admitted to "good" society in clubs. The humorist, however, makes of it a criticism of all of Jewish society:

Pharao.

. . . There is game with cards called Poker. . . . This enticing game was indulged in to a frightful excess by the younger and even the older Israelites of that day. . . . Now these youthful but sadly profligate Hebrews did nothing in their leisure hours, but play at poker. . . .[70]

Social criteria demanded that the Jew transform his behavior; the Jew knew that society expected a change of his mores in return for his newly won riches. The continuous movement, always to new places, resulting from his economic rise—"uptown" in the city and to new resorts in the summer—the continuation of his struggle for social status, is mirrored by humor:

Tschobplotz: Vas you going to dake your family to Rock-away Peach again dis Summer?
Summerpanz: No; I go by Long Pranch. I moved my shtore on Broadway, now.[71]

Suddenly, escaping from the old theme of restrictions against and non-admission of the Jew, the humorist does a somersault and plays him up as an exclusionist against the Gentile in the summer resort. The grotesqueness of this turn cannot be missed:

Exclusive.

Mitzeheimer: Goin' Long Pranch down py dis summer, Yakey?
Co Henn: Nein, not much. Dey led an Amerigan in von ohf der pest hodels last weeg.[72]

Finally, the snobbery of one Jew toward the other because of his laxity in excluding Gentiles, although not genuine from a humorous viewpoint is, nevertheless, brought up:

Snubbed.

Mrs. Hinkelheimer (slightly nearsighted): I dhinks me I will not bow to dot Meesder Ockstein. He was geddin' too familiar mit dem Chentiles alreatty.[73]

In spite of such occasional deviations, rejection of the Jew by the Gentile remains the big thing in humor. The following poem, in which the hard-pressing Jew is rejected, is remarkable also in that it was published (in 1872) in California, and shows a Californian setting. At that time the West Coast was believed to be rather far from the snobbish exclusionism of the rest of America. Even more astonishing is the fact that in the poem the counterpart of the Jew is, of all persons—a bishop! The mere personal description of the two gives away, in advance, the only possible solution to a meeting between them:

> In eighteen hundred and seventy-two
> There sailed together a bishop and Jew.
> The bishop was long, and good-looking withal,
> The Jew was mean-looking, and ugly, and small—
> His English was bad, his manners were worse,
> But he hinted his strength was a lengthy purse.
> He believed but little of holy writ,
> And never was known to lavish a bit;
> His nose had the orthodox Jewish hook,
> And his whole get-up had a Hebrew look. . . .

Naturally the Gentile refuses even to be compared with the Jew:

> "My father is Gentile, my mother too,
> And I haven't a trace in my blood of a Jew; . . .
> . . . the comparison is odious"[74]

SNUBBED.

Mrs. Hinkelheimer *(slightly near-sighted).*— I dhinks me I vill not bow to dot Meesder Ockstein. He vas geddin' too familiar mit dem Chentiles alreatty.

Snubbed *(Puck,* Vol. 26, 1889/90, p. 440).

In comparison, self-comparison or non-comparison, the rejection of the Jew sticks.

As to the treatment of communal institutions or endeavors of the Jews in American humor, one can only say that the interest in them was rather small. In letters of John Watts (1762–1765) we find the designation "the Synagogue" jokingly applied to the total of all Jews in New York, doing business there. The "Synagogue well,"[75] or "Synagogue not very well"[76] designate the state of the business deals of the Jews of New York. A general New York charity, not initiated by Jews, may be caricatured as "The old Clo' Charity" if the distribution of clothing takes place from a Jewish clothing store, Mr. Levi the owner.

The theme of general charity gains some breadth if its insufficiency as practiced by religious denominations is mocked, the humorist here singling out the Jew at the right time. He is cognizant of the manner in which a person seeking help is passed from one denomination to the other. When a poor widow is sent around from one clergyman to the other until she finally lands at a rabbi's, the following description of the situation is given:

Starving widow: Where can I go for help?
Rev. Mr. Creamcheese: You will find the Israelite Society for the Succor of the Poor at No. — Beach Street. Possibly they will attend to you.
Scene Third.—Office of the *Israelite Society for the Succor of the Poor.*
Rabbi Ben Levi in attendance. *Starving Widow* tells her tale.
Rabbi Ben Levi: Dot vas pad—it vas a case which vas very sorrowful. But I vas got, by the py-laws auf our society, to ask you a question.
Starving Widow: Well, Sir?
Rabbi Ben Levi: Vas you a Hebrew?
Starving Widow: No, Sir.
Rabbi Ben Levi: Vas your husband a Hebrew?
Starving Widow: No, Sir.

Rabbi Ben Levi: Vas your barents, any auf them, Hebrews?
Starving Widow: No, Sir.
Rabbi Ben Levi: Dot seddles id. I vas not able to assist you. Dis society vas for the aid auf Hebrews only. But ve vos sometimes above the consideration of sects. You say you vas got dwo babies?
Starving Widow: I have, Sir.
Rabbi Ben Levi: Den take this picture-book. It vas galled "The Advendares auf Ikey Isaacs in Jerusalem." It vos a nice pook, und it vill pring them great bleasure vhen dey grow up to read id. By the vay, my goot woman, dere vas a relief association not far away called the Samaritan Society. You goes dere. Here, I gife you the address.[77]

Nevertheless, Jewish charity may have impressed the humoristic observer with serious thought. We learn this from the poetic confession of another widow who, again in 1872, visits the "Ebrew Benevolent Ball . . . in Platitude Hall." After describing all the platitudes, carriages, women's dresses and jewels, and imagining discussions with rabbis on the dietary laws, she nevertheless follows up with a conclusion of deeper meaning:

But this I vill say, that the 'Ebrews is kind to the
poor and the friendless and let Christians bear in mind
Ven they gets into debt and their rent hoverdoo,
The only vun with money to 'elp 'em is the Jew,
And but for circumcision and sleepin' in de boosum
Of Abraham before 'alf the Christians I'd choose 'em."[78]

Many earnest natures, in view of communal Jewish charity work may have felt the same way. The humorist, however, like any other man, has his vested interest in the subject treated, in the poetical widow just as well as in other subjects. In these cases, the profession has a routine exit, at least where it can illustrate the subject in a drawing. A benign, serious text is added to a drawing in which all Jews are drawn in a caricaturistic manner. Thus, for instance, in the case of a charity caricature (Hilton's offer to the Jewish charity organization) titled "What are you giving us," an accusation is made against Hilton in the text; nevertheless, at the same time the caricature shows strongly exaggerated Jewish figures, promenading in front of A. T. Stewart's Department Store.[79]

What are you giving us? (*Puck*, Vol. 4, 1878/79, No. 94, p. 1).

CHAPTER 7

Family Life and Education

Wherever the humorist discovers features of Jewish society that he can exploit and depict, it is apparent that the basis of that society is the consolidated and peculiar Jewish family. Without full concentration on reflecting the Jewish family for his audience, his humor would, in time, dry up; with it, his theme is virtually inexhaustible. So convinced is he of this, that, in his creations, he includes every possible situation of family life, choosing indiscriminately and insensitively, wandering from the cradle to the grave, with marriage the milestone of the lives of his subjects. In the end, however, the Jew is proven to be a family father only through the education he gives his sons. In his fierce world, the education of women is apparently forgotten, and is represented only occasionally by the useful advice the head of the family gives his spouse.

It is a finding of deep cultural and historical meaning that the Jewish family, with its strange life, is the only source of ethnic humor that entered the American scene as a family; and that, moreover, outside of the realm of the Jewish family, family scenes in American humor are not only rare, but when they are shown, they are colorless. The humorist of the time

108

AN ECONOMICAL MEASURE.

LITTLE ISAACS.— Fader, I vants some moneys; mein slade is gracked.

FATHER ISAACS.— Mein sohn, dimes vas hardt. Use der odder site.

An economical measure *(Puck,* Vol. 23, 1887/88, p. 363).

found no family educator except in the Jew, and didn't reveal an attachment to family of any other group comparable to that which he found in the Jewish group. Again, it is Jakey Einstein who is apostrophized in this respect:

> Fond of Mrs. Einstein and
> Her too-numerous infant band
> Ever willing they should share
> Your enjoyment everywhere. . . .[1]

His parental pride shows up in the caricature "The accumulative instinct,"[2] and the good life of the whole family in a further one, "Lavishness at Hockstein's."[3] The mere staying together of the family in "Not sufficiently specific,"[4] is already enough to spur the artist to create a caricature.

When it is time to find a permanent relationship to the opposite sex, the mating of Jews is, for the humorist, the concern only of men, and is decided only in accord with the business categories of the male world. "Cigars vs. Clothing" may be the heading of an engagement announcement, in which the betrothal of "Rebekka Rosenheimer to Levi Sulzbacher" is the subject. The course of the first family evening of a prospective new husband-and-wife team is narrated in a corrupt German-Jewish-English dialect,[5] an idiom which is, to be sure, the unifying business speech of the two branches of economy that come together at this juncture.

Sentimentality at such an event is customarily eliminated; wherever its touch breaks through it is measured by the humorist with the habitual yardstick:

> Our Israelite friends have sometimes been accused of lugging the idea of money into every sort of conversation. This is not always the case. In front of a Lexington Avenue residence, one evening this week, a young man said tenderly to his girl: "Well, we are at last enkaget. And it is so sweet that I to not even look at the cost."[6]

THE ACCUMULATIVE INSTINCT.

OCKSTEIN *(coming home)*. — Aha! at lasd I geds me der prightesd, preddiesd baby in ter vorld!

BABY OCKSTEIN. — Scharge him rent vile he holts me, Mudder.

The accumulative instinct *(Puck,* Vol. 24, 1888/89, p. 202).

"Shylock vs. Wedlock"[7] therefore doesn't start only in young married life; rather, its chimes are already heard at the wedding. At the wedding ceremony, the assessment is not made in relation to the golden-pure will for matrimonial bliss, but is, in a very prosaic manner, led to the question of the genuineness of the wedding ring:

At Miss Ahrenheim's Wedding.

Ahrenheim père: Here ish der acid, Leah. Drop a liddle on der ring to see uf it was reel gold.[8]

Whenever married people have to say something to one another it is always to the same point. As a mobile object of value the wife enjoys sincere esteem. "Buy your dry goods of Cohen" is a fitting inscription on her back—revealed by the décolletage of her new gown—if he has to go with her to an expensive ball:

At the daughters of Rebecca reception.

Cohen: Dot dress cosd me eighdy-five tollars, Rachel, unt ve musd get der monish pack some vays.[9]

Whereas dangers are met by the spouses together, there is also a comfort shared by the two, as for instance in a shipwreck:

"Oh, Isaac! ain't awful?" "Yes; but ain't yer glad now dat we didn't buy first-class tickets, Rachel?"[10]

The temptations of married people do not show up in the Jewish family circle, insofar as the humorist deals with the reality of Jewish married life in America. The death of a husband leaves behind a widow who is full of understanding of her husband's past life:

AT MISS AHRENHEIM'S WEDDING.

AHRENHEIM *père.* — Here ish der acid, Leah. Drop
a liddle on der ring to see uf it vas reel golt!

At Miss Arenheim's wedding *(Puck,* Vol. 24, 1888/89, p. 117).

He was resigned.

Mrs. Abrams: An' so your poor tear husbant ees det. Vas he resignet?

Mrs. Isaacs: Yah, he vas villing to go. He said dere vas no moneys in der cloding peesiness nowatays.[11]

In family life, too, the Jew's hopes and despairs are written as a general money accounting, and a settlement with fate is sought for, as if with a hard businessman. Very little may be expected in the way of comfort or mercy as we can see from the following story:

From a stock market point of view.

Ah, Jacob, I fear I hafe not many tays to live.

Nonsense, Fader, you have as much as t'irty years yet pefore you.

Noh, Jacob, no! The Lord isn't going to take me at 100 when he can get me at 70.[12]

And where accounting cannot help, it is understood, at least, by:

Posthumous Realization.

Chipinone: I understand Solomon Isaacs died suddenly. What was the cause?

Ukerdek: Some one told him that his life insurance would expire next day.[13]

The attitude of the Jew in moments of danger, when he thinks of saving what may be saved, is likewise a continuous object of the caricaturist's art:

Jacob's Opportunity.

Mr. Himmelstein (who was first to get over): Run *toward* de bull, Chakob! Vave your redt handkercheef! And you, Rachel, come dis vay! Chakob ish der von to be tossed— he has der live-insurance![14]

FROM A STOCK MARKET POINT OF VIEW.

" Ah, Jacob, I fear I hafe not many tays to live."
" Nonsense, Fader, you have as much as t'irty years yet pefore you."
" No, Jacob, no ! The Lord is n't going to take me at 100 when he can get me at 70."

From a stock-market point of view *(Puck*, Vol. 25, 1889, p. 226).

115

But figuring out the risk and indemnification for pain is not always possible; in such cases intuition decides:

Trade Instinct at Lake George.

Mrs. Co Henn is going down for the third time.
Mr. Co Henn (who can't swim a stroke): As you loaf me, Leah, t'row dem erringks ashore! Dey gan't pe madched in der cidys![15]

The outsider, who cannot understand the true love of a husband, always has his explanation on hand:

Narrowly escaped loss.

The life-saver at Bartonhurst saved Mrs. Cohen from drowning.
"Did Cohen reward him?"
"Yes. Gave him five dollars."
"Good. He must be fonder of his wife than we thought."
"Oh' it wasn't that. She had her diamonds on."[16]

As the Jewish family is the only one generally treated in American humor, it is also exclusively Jewish education the humorist chooses as a target if he wants to show the nursery as a preschooling for life. The Pestalozzi image of education as the garden before the house in which the young plants are nursed tenderly and raised by the father, becomes in this case deliberately perverted. What happens in the house is the only substance of the child-plant's education in the garden, and the gardener-father doesn't rest before this education bears fruit.

Such training, as formulated in the caricature "Early Education,"[17] must proceed without delay as there is no time to lose: If the prenatal stage is by-passed, it is only to come more speedily to the infant. The old theme of caricature "Israëlchen has swallowed a ducat,"[18] is naturalized in America by the substitution of a ten-cent piece. In a paradoxical way the loss becomes smaller when a silver dollar is concerned:

GREAT EXPECTATIONS.

IKEY GOLDSTEIN.— Papa, I vos eighdt years oldt to-day.

MOSES GOLDSTEIN.— So you vos, mine leedle poy; so you vos.

IKEY.— Gif me a bresent, Papa?

MOSES.— Vait until it schnows, Ikey, and your papa vill make you some nice, beeg, roundt, vite, coldt schnow-palls!

Great expectations *(Puck*, Vol. 32, 1892/93, p. 269).

Mrs. Ikelstein: "Ron mit der doctor, k'vick, Solomon!
Ter paby is swallow't a silver tollar!"
Mr. I.: "Vos it dot von I lefd on der dable?"
"Yes, dot vos id. Hurry mit der doctor."
"Don'd get oxcited, Rachel, it was gounderveid."[19]

The old European fable of Jewish education whereby the
child doesn't learn anything excepting how to count money
is elaborated on in a psychological way. "Getting him interested"[20] describes the method of teaching the child how to
count by counting money instead of apples. That play is
serious to the child is recognized by the father who demonstrates to the mother, with pride, the inherited features
already visible in the child:

His natural bent.

Father (in high glee): Vell, Repecka, unt vat do you t'ink
ohf our Ikey now. Look ad him. He's put on mine coat
unt vest to make him look like a man, unt den got dree
lemons for a sign, unt he's shtarted a pawnbroker's shtore,
on der sidewalk. Mark mein vords, he'll haf der clothes
off them Christian poys' packs before dey goes away.[21]

The child's intelligence, however, emancipates him; out of
imitation of the father and his paraphernalia grows an
independent concept of economic matters:

A serious difficulty.

Mrs. Isaacs: Vot vos all you boys quarreling apoud?
Ikey: Vell, ve vanted to play ve vos forming a trusdt, but
nopody vanted to be der gustomers.[22]

When the time comes for books to enter the life of a
child , the father sets a personal example of shunning books.[23]
And when "Liddle Shakey" wants to read exciting things
about "marvelous rogues" the father furnishes him copies
of magazine advertisements.[24]

Financial *(Life,* Vol. 17, 1891, p. 233).

The result: Early education directed towards the right assessment of the value of things in money produces a blasé attitude of the child vis-à-vis less valuable presents:

Not built that way.

Rosenbaum: Vat do you think. I gave my son, Bennie, two cent for his birthday and he turn up his nose ad it.
Rosenstein: Imbossible![25]

Later, for the purpose of Junior's admission to society, indoctrination of firm rules is necessary, first of all about the criteria of the Jew in that society:

Father, what is an Israelite?

"My son, an Israelite is a rich Jew."
"And what is a Jew, my father?"
"A poor Israelite."[26]

Moving freely on the ground of that society, the Jew nevertheless may come to a fall, as in the following where he will convince himself of the indestructibility of values:

Isidor Cohen (to Lemuel Cohen, who has fallen during the last quadrille): "Wot you be so clumsy for and disgrace der family? You are der laughin'-stock of der room."
Lemuel: "Sh-h-h-! You vasn't half fly, Isidor. I vanted to feel if dot carpet vas a *real* Agsminister.[27]

In the full seriousness of the last matters in life a father has to set in order for his son that consideration of the realities takes first place:

Mr. Isaacs: Now Esau, I haf made my will and left everything I have to you.
Esau: Yes, vader!
Mr. Isaacs: Yes, and as you get all the benefits, I'll keep the cost of making the will out of your next week's salary.[28]

Indeed, such a final arrangement may be taken as the conclusion of an education received.

the boar. From
the clock struck

H. W. Phillips.

THE SON'S RAISE

The son's raise *(Life*, Vol. 27, 1896, p. 451).

CHAPTER 8

Art and the Theatre

O BJECTS OF ART to be kept as ornaments in the house were only of small importance at a time when the upper crust of the Jewish merchant class in the country was struggling to be formed. A real salon as a meeting place where the lady could have paraded her art treasures was almost non-existent. The relationship of the Jew to objects of art in the home is therefore mirrored in humor only rarely, and the art collector as a snob is entirely lacking. Nevertheless, we find the theme of the beginnings of a Jewish salon used to a certain extent. Wherever wealth came into existence, and luxury apartments were furnished with refined objects, the urge to represent riches in the setting of such things was a subject for mockery: The satire "I invite a famous person" (Ich lad mir eine Beruhmtheit ein)[1] reflects this urge in a city of the West, and the point of this satire is that only the old acquaintances show up, and no new visitor is found who could advertise the treasures of the newly rich.

Deriding Jewish mores extends also to the small things of the salon insofar as they intend to represent objects of art as if they were souvenirs:

122

A CASE FOR GERRY.

Mr. Hockstein.—Sol has peen a naughty poy and I'm going to punish him.

Mrs. Hockstein.—Vot you do mit him?

Mr. Hockstein.—I vos going to put him on der gounter and make him vatch me vile I scharge der next gustomer only six per cent.

Mrs. Hockstein *(in motherly horror).*—Oh, Fadder! You vos *too* cruel!

A case for Gerry *(Puck*, Vol. 32, 1892/93, p. 348).

The Misses Oppenheimer of New York, gave a German on Thursday evening which was led by Mr. Ikey Solomons, of the great clothing house on the Bowery. The favors were very handsome and unique, the ladies receiving pawn tickets which, upon presentation at the supper-room, entitled the bearer to a plate of ice-cream, and the gentlemen getting little cigarette cases with the words "50% off for cash" embroidered on the covers in old-gold letters.[2]

Artistically valuable humorous drawings of happenings in Jewish salons, by Charles Dana Gibson only appeared later.[3]

On the other hand, portraiture, practiced by individual Jewish artists, and the patronage of this art through the portraits that Jews ordered, was known widely and also (already in 1851) parodied:

I believe one of the movers in this business is, without doubt, clever in his profession—he is to paint a fine picture, historical, though certainly portrait-painting is his forte. The subject is to be "The Pharisee and the Publican." I doubt not, as a *historical* picture, it will be one of his best—especially as his former acquaintance with the latter denomination of persons may cause him to give a pleasant *patronizing* air to the Publican. No doubt the artist will bring in a sort of *ideal* likeness of himself, as he did once before, they say, in a celebrated picture.[4]

In the so-called salon we also find a weak indication of gallantry. In the caricature, "A millionaire magnet. The attraction of gold"[5] we see the Jewish rich surrounded by women.

The figure of the Jewish art dealer was also a familiar one by this time. In the caricature "The old masters—and how they are put on the market"[6] we see the paradox that objects of art, instead of being exhibited in the home of the Jew, serve him as a means of earning a living. In one case, the artist himself is imported and works in the display-window of the store painting Japanese vases. The exploitation of this caricature by the humorist, however, would not

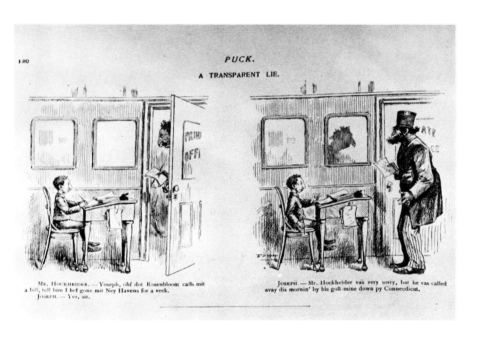

A transparent lie *(Puck*, Vol. 26, 1889/90, p. 120).

have been complete had there not been a hint of education
at the same time:

Following the movement.

Bloomenfeld: Vat's der use mit Leo taking art insdrugtions
by dot Goober Insditude, ofd dem was not abblied by
some bractical usefulness, alretty?[7]

Ignorance in matters of art served for deriding the prospective Jewish female buyer as well. In one of the rare
instances where the Jewish female is permitted to decide an
economic matter, her ignorance lets her down:

An eye witness.

Mrs. Newman: "Will you guarantee that this picture was
really painted by Holbein?"
Ikenstein: Madam, I saw him paint it meinself, ven I
vos a boy, in Chermany."[8]

In entirely different spheres, and in disproportionately
larger dimensions, appears the mirroring of the Jew as per-
former on the stage, becoming a unique performance in
itself: the caricaturing of the Jewish "theatre trust." In
this case, satire becomes deeply earnest and the humorist
loosens a full emotional discharge in which he loses his
uninvolved point of view. In this frontier region professional
envy of competitors unscrupulously sought a victim by bringing an imagined underdog to the forefront of the public's
consciousness. Cleverly connected with this manoeuver was
the hated subject of the trust, which had already, by this time,
become an object of social criticism. Historically, there was
talk of a "Jewish" trust in America before in a single case,
the lease of the exclusive right to hunt seal in the Pribylow
Islands by the Alaska Commercial Company (1869), was
conceded to this company by agreement with the American
government.[9] However, at that time the storm against "Jewish monopoly" moved mainly in the commercial circles of

The attraction of gold *(Puck,* Vol. 9, 1881, p. 116).

California, and did not even create a ripple among humorists. In the case of the theatre, however, it was entirely different. Here all things were combined: The stereotype of the Jew could be brought to the stage; furthermore the Jew as an actor could be derided; finally, the most urgent of all the theatre problems, the relationship of the omnipotent impresario and the theatre firm could be found. (Vis-à-vis this headache, even the Jewish journalist as a professional theatre critic played no role at all.)

The first responsibility for things as they are was allotted to the general Jewish theatre public, and it is said without any humor:

> . . . They do not know the vulgar New York Jew, . . . his uneducated fondness for the theatre is largely responsible for the wretched productions which are sent to other parts of the country as "New York successes," only to be rejected by communities where higher standards prevail. He and his women-folk form a large percentage of the New York population which spends its money in public places, and in theatrical affairs he cuts a wide swathe, indeed.[10]

All in all the theatre is not much more than a Jewish matter and is also seen by New Yorkers in this fashion. In the following we have it from a child's mouth, again in an educational scene:

Correct.

Teacher: What are the two principal events of the Jewish year?
Bright New York Boy: The Feast of Passover, and the opening of the dramatic season.[11]

That the Jew is omnipresent in the theatre, on the stage, in the orchestra and in the onlooker's hall, not to speak of its management, is shown in the cartoon "The Hebraization of the American Drama. For further details just look in at almost any New York theatre."[12]

The Hebraization of the American Drama *(Life*, Vol. 22, 1893, pps. 412-13).

With such a theatre public filling the diamond horseshoe of his imagination, a humorist-theatre critic wrote as follows:

> A more brilliant audience *than that which* the *first* performance of *"Diplomacy"* at the Empire Theatre has *rarely* assembled in New York. It was brilliant in more senses than one, and so many diamonds were in evidence that several estimable Jewish ladies and gentlemen have become permanently cross-eyed through their efforts to see all the jewels at once.
> The Syndicate passed on all applications for seats, with the result that there were present very few persons who were not objectionable.

He further elaborated on this theme of the behavior of the "not objectionables" and crowned the whole scene with the concluding words of his competitor, the Jewish theatre critic:

> Mr. Isidor Cohn who attends all the first nights at the Empire, says he has seldom seen a finer audience. He also remarked that there were very few Christians present.[13]

On a broader front, the attack is diverted from the Jewish public to the performance itself, and support is sought above all outside of New York. Letters are published, directed against bad performances in the West:

> . . . this rotten company [Frohman] has played at "robber prices." Even in the West your fight against the Israelite syndicate is appreciated.[14]

The matter is not improved when the program agrees with "higher" taste:

> *Everyman* is produced at Mendelssohn Hall with an attempt to provide surroundings different from those of the ordinary theatre. This is a shallow pretense, of course, when one stops to think that its Christian teachings are

set forth under Jewish managers simply as a money-making venture. . . .[15]

The cartoon "Ophelia," directed against the advertisement of the new program put out by the Jewish theatre owners, gives this explanation:

> On the adjacent scenery may be observed the budding of an idea already adopted by certain American (!) Theatrical Managers.[16]

The entire American theatre scene appears as something unnatural; gigantic native powers and artistic potentialities are suppressed by small minds. In the caricature "Gulliver Knickerbocker and the Lilliputians" appears the native giant fettered by "Diam.(onds) Real Estate, Theatrical Trust." "New Jerusalem, formerly New York, for sale. Hebrews only"[17] is the result. Finally, when it comes to the men of the theatrical enterprise, their names known all over America, their arrival from no man's land is the first thing mocked at. The caricature "In Retrospect" shows them furnished with peddlers' boxes, selling jumping jacks.[18] Their methods, even if accompanied by the success of a play, are of course only the methods of the "Old Clo':"

> . . . The whole business only furnishes further proof that Baxter Street methods are altogether too prevalent in theatrical affairs and "Mr. Frohman presents them."[19]

Such Baxter Street methods are nailed down in a long tirade:

> If a Christian wants to by him a seat der cashier in der box office tells him der ain't none but on der sidewalk outside dere is von of Charlie's men who has plenty of seats vor two dollars and a helluf abiece, and Charlie makes him helluf a dollar more on each seat he sells to a Christian.[20]

In respect to the plays performed, the genuine American drama is portraited in a cartoon as the "leading lady" chained by the Jewish theatre entrepreneurs.[21] Any educational value is denied to these plays. The caricature "The theatrical trust as educator"[22] shows Jews, producers and public, with no art program in sight. As a contrast to this appears Shakespeare as a visitor on Broadway in the cartoon "A distinguished visitor."[23]

It goes without saying, that where a Shakespeare is banned, an American theme which was then becoming a classic could never make its way to the stage:

> The beginning dramatist who should try to sell "Uncle Tom's Cabin" to a New York manager today would get a large part of experience. He couldn't sell his play. That goes without saying. He would learn a lot about Jew dialect, a Jew insolence which he might incorporate in some later drama but he wouldn't find a producer for "Uncle Tom's Cabin. . . ."[24]

As for the personnel in the theatre business, it is accused of employing only Jews, "everyt' is Kosher eggzept der actors."[25]

And the actors are non-Jews only because there are no important Jewish actors, "so Charlie has to hire Christians;" whoever offends him is, in addition, placed on a blacklist:

> Efery day you can see actors without overcoats and who only eat twice a week just because Charlie hef got 'em on his black list.[26]

The Trust also cares for the rising generation. In the cartoon "The Syndicate School of Acting. Situations Guaranteed" we see the Jewish theatre director raising marionettes from a box. "Salary 10 dollars per week" is guaranteed them. In the corner the genuine actor (male and female figures) are depicted, terrified by the new turn of events.[27]

A distinguished visitor *(Life,* Vol. 27, 1896, pps. 11-12).

133

This domination of the theatre is maintained by two factors: the first is the "special Hebrew Padrone . . . New Jerusalem Stage Syndicate . . . can hope to attain Mosaic patronage . . ."[28] The second is the omnipotent press:

> All he does is to put some show-pils on der fences and some small adverteizements in der bapers and den der Kosher baper and der Kosher fellows what writes vor die udder bapers says Charlie Frohman has got a good show and der Christians come and gif up deir good dollars to Charlie.[29]

At this point, the criticism leveled at the theatre enterprise leads to Jewish journalism, whose mirror in wit and graphic humor represents a separate chapter.

Broadway's conquest by the Jewish theatre impresarios, however, didn't harmonize with the actors' superstition that a church building, transformed into a theatre, always goes bankrupt. It sometimes happened that occurrences of this sort did take place on Broadway, but Jewish impresarios seemed to be exempt from this spell when they "chained" American drama. In reverse—a theatre turned into a church brought good luck to the new undertaking—according to the same superstition. One paper gave as the reason for this that apparently the preachers are better actors than their colleagues on the stage.

Personal jealousy as well as gossip in the actors' world with all its paranoia, are likewise ascribed to the "syndicate;" competition for roles in plays appears as a fight for personal freedom. "Pleasant spectacle for the new century" is so described by *Metcalfe* in a review of the play "Mistress Nell."[30] Even ambiguities in respect to actresses may be found. "My success was largely due to my Israelite manager" is the title of a caricature of this manager in the "Memoirs of an Actress."[31]

However, the whole specter of the Jewish theatre is wiped away in a vision of a "National Theater endowment by Andrew Carnegie." In the cartoon "Hasten the day," the theatre Jews are horrified that Carnegie's millions are now invested in the theatre business, and the American drama itself is hardly able to believe in the good fortune of its sudden liberation from the Jews.[32]

A special phenomenon likewise accessible to caricature, although to a lesser degree was:

Racial Impersonation.

The stage Jew . . . is impersonated . . . not only in his ridiculous aspects but in his vicious ones. His greed, his avarice, his grasping qualities, . . . have been faithfully pictured, as well as his peculiarities of dress, manner and speech. . . . The character of *Hoggenheimer,* played by a Jew, laughed at by audiences in which there were many Jews, and exploited for the money there was in it, under the favoring auspices of the Theatrical Trust, . . .[33]

The *circulus vitiosus,* the vicious circle, whereby the Jew, derided by a fellow Jew, brings money to the theatre entrepreneur from Jewish onlookers, somewhat mollified the mood of the critic, but was not followed up by him. In the Jewish press, matters naturally were seen in a very different light; a cry of "slander!" was raised there.[34] Ocassionally, dignified rejections of outspoken Jewish roles may also be found in the general press.[35]

With the edge of the thorny theatre problem removed, Jews, even of the lowest station in life, remained devoted to the theatre. Even where this devotion is not "bizz," the Jew is an eager onlooker, warming himself at the thought of theatre personalities. His enthusiasm at meeting one of them in real life likewise constituted a source of humor, for instance in a sketch of 1851, where the pawnbroker's family sees the adored actor enter their store:

I vanted to see you very mooch. I saw you blay at the teatre lasht night and I want to present you wid a peautiful Charman flute.[36]

CHAPTER 9

Journalism and Politics

In AMERICA the popular image of journalism and newspapers was derived from the image of the one-man frontier editor. In mining camp and muddy frontier towns as well as in young cities he was of the earliest pioneers, a neighbor known to all as a seeker after news for his paper through personal relationships with people. As such he also entered American literature, often described, but frequently himself a master of literary humor, critically observing the life in all the new settlements. There were almost no national figures among the news distributors if we discount those journalists who achieved political fame. None of them had been known for inventing a new method of publishing the news. The best known Jewish journalist of frontier times was Edmund Rosewater in Omaha, instrumental in putting up Lincoln as a candidate for the presidency, at the same time an editor of the old school. Of him it was said that he was the news-paperman most beaten by dissatisfied readers. Otherwise, the role of the Jews in American newspaper life was rather a modest one, and important only in the German American press.

136

The revolutionary change in journalism of basing the paper on sensational news, was connected by contemporaries with the name of Joseph Pulitzer. To characterize this new man significantly Jewish symbols were used, although Pulitzer was only partly of Jewish descent. Once again, the uncontainable news, reporting the economic situation as well as the general news, could be explained to the masses of men in no other way than by the appearance of the Jew on a new American scene. Those who, in an excess of zeal saw the fine Jewish hand in everything new, arrived immediately at a new comparison with other segments of social life:

> The Theatrical Syndicate has done to debase dramatic art in America what Mr. Pulitzer has done for American Journalism by the discovery of yellow methods.[1]

According to the humorist, the new method consists in the art of making a physical clamor with the news and, in addition, of manipulating it at will. As the former, Pulitzer is caricatured as the possessor of the trumpet, "Daily Sensation;"[2] as the latter he appears as a juggler turning a balloon with his feet inscribed "world."[3]

The personality attributed to the man, Pulitzer, as a Jew, is in accord with all the contemporary notions of Jews: physically, by drawing his Jewish nose in the usual, exaggerated fashion;[4] he wears a "Jewish" hat of the Middle Ages, recalling the position of the Jew in the medieval world, and is furnished with a spear. The latter suggests the word "Judenspiess" (Jewish spear), the medieval symbol for the Jew's taking interest on loans. This paraphernalia shows up in a cartoon where all the other medieval contemporaries are only carrying helmets, and no other figure carries a spear.[5] The Jewish hat was to follow Pulitzer repeatedly in later caricatures.[6]

But to be truly modern and of our time, the symbol of the Jew's new economic station in life must also be used. Pulitzer carries a traveling bag, like a peddler's pack on his

Cleveland's entry into Washington *(Puck,* Vol. 17, 1885, pps. 8-9).

back, with a tag bearing his name. Of all the people depicted in this cartoon "Busted," he is again the only one drawn with this symbol.[7]

To make a mistake about what the new journalism represents is impossible; even the printer's devil and the proofreaders are in on the joke:

No mistake.

"There was a bad mistake in the paper this morning," said the news editor to the proofreader. "In referring to the death of this man Linnere, the types say that he was prominent in the new Jerusalem."
"Well?"
"It should have been the New Journalism."
"Oh," said the proofreader, "I don't know that there's much difference."[8]

The ambitions and aspirations of the new journalism are, as described, to have the world as a stage, as the world court and the world government. In the cartoon "Puck's dream of an ideal government," Pulitzer appears as "Editor of World—Supreme Judge."[9] The responsibility for such huge tasks is gigantic. Classical mythological images help to carry it as in the cartoon "Atlas Joe; or the fearful responsibilities of a self-appointed manager of the Universe," in which Pulitzer, actually carrying the globe, gives his instructions in all directions.[10]

But, once again, the endless originates in the finite, daily politics precede eschatological matters; the caricature then shows Pulitzer at his daily work. In "No welcome for the little stranger" he is drawn hanged with "The World," in a situation where he meets resistance.[11] To conquer this resistance, esthetic measures are not out of line which are meant to give his yellow press a new look. In the cartoon "Time to clean up, boys and look pretty"[12] he is shown washing his hands. A number of his political concoctions are

Puck's dream of an ideal government (*Puck*, Vol. 26, 1889/90, p. 140).

judged to be detrimental; In "The unsuccessful Alchemists" he is shown trying various combinations.[13] Other daily events bring "Valentines social and political," showing Pulitzer boxing with Dana.[14] As his power grows, he tries himself also as a kingmaker: "Another presidential fishing party" shows him as an angler.[15] But he may also be one of the King's rebels. In the cartoon "Columbus Cleveland and his mutinous crew"[16] he appears among the mutineers.

The new press is one of the factors responsible for the new complications. "The Yellow Pest—Putting its nose into everything," shows us Pulitzer carrying "Yellow Journal War Plans."[17] Where he shows his hand in the internal politics of the country, the noise is likewise the main thing. "No party lines when the national honor is in peril" draws him as a gunner firing the "Sound Money Press."[18]

An outstanding theme is that Pulitzer is always busy, "A worker—not a striker,"[19] and therefore always in the picture. He is never forgotten, a fact to which the multitude of humorous drawings of which he is the subject, bears testimony; drawings with and without antisemitic themes, often even without any political background; where he serves, by his mere presence, the purpose of caricatures of other themes, especially those illuminating social situations.[20]

Finally, we land in the pseudo-eschatological, showing Pulitzer as an equal among equals, toiling for salvation in the vineyard of the Lord. The provocative cartoon says it in strong words: "The spiritual salvation army is doing good work,—now let us have a social salvation army." In the drawing we see Pulitzer sitting at the editor's desk, hanging on the wall is a poster, "Daily sensation."[21] The signal, "All aboard the millenium," to be sure, was given at that time for everyone.[22]

In the gallery of American so-called Judases, Joseph Pulitzer occupies a unique position. He represents the only Judas of Jewish descent, and, in addition, one for whom Jews, neither of the olden times nor of the last generation in

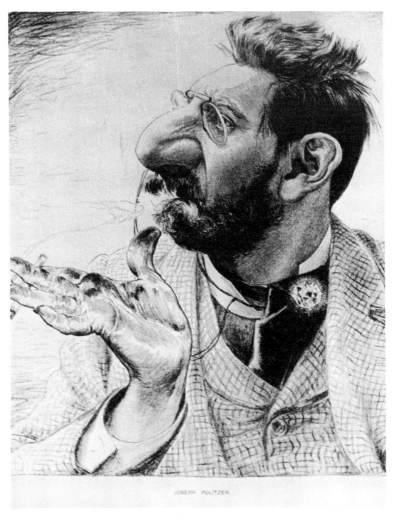

"Joseph Pulitzer" *(Life,* Vol. 30, 1897, p. 459).

America, bear any responsibility. The *Sun*, for which J.P. meant simply Jew Pulitzer, stated:

> The Jews of New York have no reason to be ashamed of Judas Pulitzer, if he has denied his race and religion. . . . The shame rests exclusively upon himself.

The statement had been preceded by reprinting an earlier article of the *Hebrew Standard* under the title: "He is a Jew who does not want to be a Jew." Naturally, points of comparison with the genuine Judas were also not omitted:

> . . . The contemporary Judas has not the sensibility of his prototype. . . .[23]

In respect to his Jewish visage, Pulitzer sets a record—although this record is somewhat softened by an apology to Jews, "his face is repulsive, not because the physiognomy is Hebraic, but because it is Pulitzeresque. . . ." Appealing to "The Wandering Jew," he is given this advice: "Move on, Pulitzer, move on," which advice is heeded mainly in caricature. Even Pulitzer's known failing eyesight is cruelly derided:

In the Office of the "Evening World."

Joseph P.: I must confess that that confounded *Evening Sun* is getting too strong for my eyes.[24]

In humor, too, the Jews as a political group are seen only in the electorate; their demands and expectations from political life don't count, first, and are mocked at afterwards. The political editor, to be sure, has a double function; aside from election times the voter exists for him also as a newspaper reader who is to be considered, and there is no doubt about the distinct group interests of the voter-reader. The caricature "The bold editor of the period. Trying to avoid the numerous toes he must *not* tread on" shows us stretched-

THE BOLD EDITOR OF THE PERIOD.

TRYING TO AVOID THE NUMEROUS TOES HE MUST NOT TREAD ON.

The bold editor of the period *(Puck,* Vol. 5, 1879, p. 53).

out feet, inscribed, "Jew," "German," and "Irish."[25] The
block vote of ethnic groups was caricatured early and the
fact that the politicians conceded the effectiveness also of a
"Jewish" vote, is recognized. The cartoon, "On to Washington,"[26] from the election of 1872, shows different groups of
voters—among them the "Hebrew Vote," inscribed on a
yellow flag, carried by a Jew.

During the election of 1888, politicians' endeavors to
organize ethnic block votes were very badly received and
nailed down in a caricature. "The Disgrace of American
Politics—Truckling to the foreign vote" shows the Jew next
to the German and the Irishman. Among the headlines
"quoted literally from the N.Y. daily papers of October and
November 1888" we find "Col. Cruger to Hebrew Americans" and "Prominent Hebrews for Harrison."[27]

Sentiment against Jews is expressed in this humorous campaign song to which an explanatory introduction is given:

> Among all the would-be campaign songs that have been
> suggested for the use of a patient population, how does it
> happen that no use has been made of the vigorous lyric
> known as "Benjamin Levi?" Here is a ringing campaign
> song, all ready made, and the people know the tune and
> yet our Republican friends have passed it scornfully by.
> Don't you seem to hear it? From Benjamin out in
> Hoosierdom,
> To Levi in New York,
> The cry is "Lift the tax from rum
> And rise the tax on cork."[28]

The Jew is here pointed out in the picture of the election
even before Election Day arrives, thus his presence among
those who seek favors from their elected president, is noted,
too. An epilogue is attached to the campaign song. The
cartoon "The threatened raid of the Harrisons upon Washington" shows a Jewish couple with the title, "Mrs. Levis
Harrissohn Baxter St. N. Y."[29] The joyful play with the

The threatened raid of the Harrisons upon Washington *(Puck*, Vol. 25, 1889, pps. 216-17).

president's name, to be sure, could not be left untouched by the humorist.

Political fraternizing with Jews was also derided as in the following:

Political Misinformation.

. . . Private Secretary Halford spread a reasonable quantity of it upon a tongue sandwich. The significant fact that he selected tongue instead of ham, is considered by the most intelligent of the correspondents as indicative of the pacific relation which the Administration is desirous of preserving with the American Hebrews. Secretary Blaine was afterward interviewed about the matter, and said that while he had not been consulted, he approved of the private secretary's action in the affair; . . .[30]

Ideas of favors politicians can grant are derided in "A new use for congressmen,"[31] where Mr. Isaacs sen. hopes for the mailing of his business circulars by congressional frank.

In the treatment of municipal politics, the old Know-Nothing complaint is warmed over whereby Jew and Irishman possess a monopoly of municipal offices. They divide them up among themselves, whereas the American of Anglo-Saxon descent is left out in the cold:

A lamentable flaw.

Alderman Dinkelspeil: Vot you tink, Moriarty, aboud de gomplexion of the new poard?
Alderman Moriarty: There's a dam'd American in it be the name of Johnson. I like it in other rispicts.[32]

Of all the Jewish politicians in the world, it is only the contemporary Disraeli who enjoys immunity from hostility in numerous drawings.[33]

As a foreign factor of financial politics, Rothschild is mentioned on certain occasions. For the celebration of American Independence, a letter from Rothschild to Grant is drawn:

A FAIR AND UNPREJUDICED JURY FOR THE "BOODLERS."

Court Judge—"Gentlemen, I believe that you have not read the papers or formed any opinion whatever. Proceed with the Trial."

A fair and unprejudiced jury *(Judge,* Vol. 11, 1886, No. 270, p. 16).

For the Centennial Celebration.

Aside from two congratulatory letters from the emperors of Germany and Austria, reported literally a few days ago, General Grant has also received the following letter: "Great and much-beloved friend! I am taking the liberty of expressing to you—although until now I have not done business with democracies—my warmest congratulations on the hundredth birthday of the great republic. Furthermore, if I may be allowed, I would like at the same time, to bring to your recollection my well-established bank and exchange business. For Your Excellency, I will charge a half percent less. Yours affectionately, Rothschild."[34]

It was ironic to set the congratulation of the money potentate, who in contemporary European caricature was drawn as the money pump of Europe, on the side of emperors. And this irony is given a still more piquant flavor through the intimation that Rothschild did not deem democracies to be worthy of credit up to that time. There was a belief circulating in New York that Rothschild, trusting the poor judgment of his agent, had speculated for too long a time on the victory of the Confederacy and had lost money by it; and that he recovered his losses later, however, with bonds of the victorious Union.

New York City's American Mayor (*Judge*, Vol. 13, 1887, No. 337, p. 16).

CHAPTER 10

Immigration

J EWISH IMMIGRATION, as a social novelty and of political
concern, creating a new object of humor, had its inception
later with the arrival of the Russian and East European Jews.
The old immigration of the German Jews was not strongly
criticized even in the years of the Know-Nothing agitation
against foreigners. The German Jew had not been pointed
out, in humor, as an immigrant. In a cartoon "The Happy
Family exhibited since 1776 in Uncle Sam's Republican
Gardens for the Instruction of Nations" (1851)[1] he appears
as a witness for the lack of problems in immigration. He
stands next to the German and other immigrants to fill out
the picture of the peaceful coexistence of the immigrant
peoples. Russian Jews, however, at the same time that they
signalized the beginnings of a new mass migration of South
and East European peoples, appeared immediately in the
mirror of humor. Their arrival takes place by way of "The
new Trans-Atlantic Hebrew Line. For the exclusive use of
the Persecuted."[2] The ship carries inscriptions in Hebrew
letters, and it swarms with Jews from the deck to the mast.

The comparison that likened Jewish and Chinese immigration, considered undignified by American Jews who

We Americans, 1620 *(Life,* Vol. 10, 1887, pps. 23-24).

shared their countrymen's other prejudices, and surely, also, doubtful politically, appears in caricature, with a clear anti-semitic point, at least once. "The Chinaman's idea of it"[3] shows Castle Garden, and Russian Jews arriving together with other immigrants. The reaction of the native population to the Russian Jewish immigration is mirrored in humor entirely spontaneously, and runs through the whole scale of feelings, from welcome to doubt and rejection. National pride speaks from the cartoon "Welcome to all!"[4] in which Uncle Sam greets all immigrants equally. The further feeling that the Jewish immigrant has to be defended against exploitation after his arrival, appears in pictures like "Castle Garden emigrant catchers"[5] and "Just as dangerous now as then."[6]

On the other hand, strangeness to the new human elements often produced queer feelings which were sometimes expressed in an unrestrained way. The following was printed in the first years of the big East European Jewish immigration (1883) and was included in a *"Household Book of Wit and Humor."*

The white squall.

> . . . Strange company was harbored
> We'd a hundred Jews at larboard,
> Unwashed, uncombed, unbarbared—
> Jews black, and brown, and gray.
> With terror it would seize ye,
> And make your souls uneasy,
> To see those Rabbis greasy,
> Who did nought but scratch and pray.
> Their dirty children puking—
> Their dirty saucepans cooking—
> Their dirty fingers hooking
> Their swarming fleas away.
> . . . Then all the fleas in Jewry
> Jumped up and bit like fury:
> And the progeny of Jacob
> Did on the main-deck wake up;

The Chinaman's idea of it *(Judge,* Vol. 2, 1882, No. 34, p. 2).

(I wot those greasy Rabbins
Would never pay for cabins;)
And each man moaned and jabbered in
His filthy Jewish gabardine,
In woe and lamentation,
And howling consternation.
And the slashing water drenches
Their dirty brats and wenches;
And they crawl from bales and benches,
In a hundred thousand stenches.[7]

Thus, it becomes rather understandable that the public opinion of the country, too, was tossed about between sympathy and antipathy for the newcomers. The Russian Jew encountered much false sympathy, true impulses of brotherly assistance—aside from talk and printed paper—were quite rare in the various countries overseas. The situation confronting the immigrants in countries other than the United States, could not be satirized better than in the following piece:

Where shall they go.

Suggestions from various sources regarding the exiled Russian Jews.

(From the *Labrador Pemmican*)

The whole civilized world stands aghast at the barbarity of the Czar, who has driven from his dominions five millions of honest hardworking people. Happily enough, if they come to this hemisphere they will find a region in which race prejudice is unknown and in whose warm climate they will cease to regret the colder latitude from which they were driven. The vast fertile plains of Brazil offer marvelous inducements to these unfortunate representatives of a great race.

(From the *Chilian Daily Nitrate*).

The banished and persecuted sons of Israel will find a warm welcome awaiting them on our hospitable shores. We need citizens of the grand old Hebrew race to develop our industries and revive the glories of our commerce.

An indiscriminating hostess *(Life*, Vol. 21, 1893, pps. 74-75).

But, unfortunately for us, the climate of Chili has too often proved fatal to those who have come here from the cold, rarified atmosphere of northern Europe. Northern Dakota presents a field for the labor of these worthy people, which it would be hard to duplicate in this hemisphere.

(From the *Mexican Vaquero*).

Religious intolerance, is, thank heaven, unknown in this country, and it is hard for us to realize that there can exist, at the close of this nineteenth century, a sovereign so brutal as to send into perpetual banishment five millions of people, whose sole fault is that they choose to worship their creator in their own way. It is peculiarly unfortunate for these people that they are unable to adapt themselves to the climate of those tropical or semi-tropical lands which would gladly welcome them. In fact, it is only in Patagonia that the wanderers will be able to find the heaven which they seek.[8]

There were also unequivocally hostile caricatures denigrating the new Jewish immigration. In the cartoon "Landing of the Pilgrims. As it might have been"[9] the future of these people is described as a prophetic vision. In it the street-peddler may be seen, and also the three balls of the pawnbroker; even the theatrical trust shows itself. The future alrightnik is shown in caricature and explained in words:

The first step.

Mosey's brudder-in-law, vot choost come ofer,—he vill get along all righdt, you bet!
"He can not shpeak the United Shtates lankwich, aindt it?"
"No; but he can gount der United Shtates moneysh!"[10]

As a kind of qualified opposition to immigrant assistance, appears the cartoon "Charity begins at home."[11] In it are shown Russian Jews at Castle Garden cared for with "Meal tickets" and "Clothing" and, on their side, unaided Missis-

Charity begins at home *(Judge,* Vol. 1, 1882, No. 22, p. 16).

sippi flood sufferers. The feelings of the latter are expressed with the words: "Oh, if we, too, were Russian Refugees!"

As soon as the new immigrant is settled under a roof, new thoughts, doubts, and accusations against him appear, inciting, in turn, general social criticism called forth by these attitudes. The most popular, in a sense the best understood picture of him, is the drawing "Uncle Sam's Tenement House,"[12] in which the Russian Jew lives symbolically together, under one roof, with all the other immigrant peoples. One of the early problems was also the use by employers of inexperienced new Jewish immigrants as scabs to break a strike. This led to collisions with the police and with the striking workers and shows up in a caricature "National Pride."[13] Further, there was a widely spread aversion to closely packed ethnic settlements of immigrant groups. The agitation against them produced an imaginary humorous picture of fenced-in religious colonies of Jews. The caricature, "Religious Colonization"[14] shows us the future of a group of Jews in a number of prophetic visions:

> If the Jews succeed—and they are an able and prolific race—what is to become of the Hog-business—outside of Cincinnati?
> . . . passing through a colony where all the trees bear triple gold balls for fruit . . . we advise all the pretty Jewish maidens to make love over the fence which divides the colonies. . . .[15]

And in a further cartoon "The Craze for religious Colonization" the "Jewish Colonization Company" is the target. We see in the picture a village where Jews milk cows and feed geese and the sign "Koscher" is hanging. It goes without saying that the "old clothes" seller is also to be found there.[16]

For some time, the fear of ethnic neighborhood settlement continued; however, as soon as it became clear that the Russian Jews were settling in the crowded close quarters of

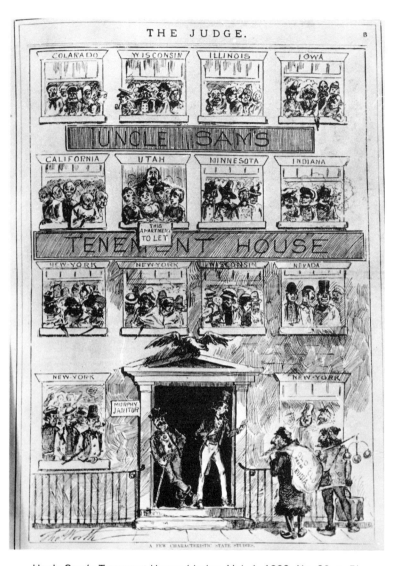

Uncle Sam's Tenement House *(Judge,* Vol. 1, 1882, No. 23, p. 5).

the city, fear of their block vote arose as a new theme for the humorist. Mr. Dooley knew how to tell it:

> There ar-re twinty thousan' Rooshian Jews at a quarther a vote in th' Sivinth ward; an', are-rimed with rag hooks, they'd be a tur-r-ble thing f'r anny inimy iv th' Anglo Saxon 'lieance to face.[17]

The end of ethnic block voting was seen as the fulfillment of a promise for America. This is shown us in the cartoon "The day we are waiting for." This day will arrive "When the 'Irish,' 'German' and all the others 'national votes' shall get together and call themselves American."[18]

The abuse of the Russian Jewish immigrant workers in the sweatshops of the city called for general attention. Here the humorist functioned not only as a social critic but also as an enlightener, laying bare the skeleton of human exploitation. In the cartoon "All a question of the scale we do it on" we see a part of a Jewish sweatshop and read under the illustrations the following commentary:

> This man, who pays starvation wages to a few clothing workers, is a "cruel and heartless sweatshop proprietor." This man, who pays starvation wages to several thousand miners, is "one of the leading coal-operators of the country."[19]

The pogrom refugee was uneasy about the possibility of living in this new country in accord with the proscriptions of his religion. He got his first unexpected enlightenment about this aspect of America in the caricature "Everything you want."

> Rosenbaum (newly landed): Can I get kosher meat in New York?
> Ikenstein: Certainly, mein frent, certainly; all kinds— you can ged kosher hams if you wand them.[20]

The day we are waiting for *(Puck,* Vol. 26, 1889/90, p. 302).

But as soon as economic success is about to be achieved, his social aspirations rise with it, and soon the humorous literature shows us that there are among them, already, well-arrived ones. In 1892, in the drawings of the New York salons, we see this new, arrived element. "At Mrs. Nathan Diamondstein's"[21] a Jewish ball shows this new layer in society already in high gear. Once the bearers of these Russian Jewish names reached the top, they no longer speak so kindly about new immigrants:

Immigration.

. . . Ike Diamondstein the Jew exclaims:
Ah, Izzy, ain't dat grandt!
Ve yangees haf such nople aims
und vill togeter standt,
Ve've got der goods, ve're nach ralized
"Americavich is civilzized.
So keep dose aliens outen!"[22]

Human tragedy is revealed to us when the rich Jew is confronted with the poor immigrant, his own fate in past times recalled to memory:

"But dot was long ago."
Two Ends of the Line.

I don't recognize him, my frent,
I ain't dot kindt of Shoo;
I own a shtore, un' bay my rent,
Und make it bay me, too.
De besht of goots are on the shelef,
Bei Moses Cohen un' Co.—
Oh, I begun like him, myself—
Bot dot vas long ako.
I vear dot lovely di'mond pin;
My son dot Sixty-Nint' is in—
Dey call him Sheeny Ike.
You bet zwei tollar un' a helef,
I'am Moses Cohen un' Co.

Is this his mission? *(Life,* Vol. 19, 1892, pps. 332-33).

> Vell, I vas vonce like dot myself
> But dot vas long ako."

It swarms now with new immigrants.[23]

Reluctance to remember turned into an active antagonism of those who have arrived against the new immigrants. At the same time, immigration became the big political issue, and its restriction was already demanded by certain groups. The anti-restrictionist cartoon "Looking backward," links these two elements. In the picture we see a new immigrant ascend the landing stage; five old immigrants, now arrived and in fine dress, hold up their hands, warding him off; but each of them sees before him a shadow of his earlier self; behind the pelted Jew, stands his ego in the first stage after his arrival— the tablet-peddler.[24] Memory, sometimes a paradise, became a visit to hell. The use of the sufferings endured by the immigrant for the enjoyment of an audience had few precedents. The humorist also had something to say, involving the Jew, concerning the new proposed immigrant tests. In the cartoon "The immigrant question," among a few solutions by *Puck's* Correspondents, is shown a Jew trying his muscular strength by lifting weights. The following lines form a commentary:

> There is only one standard for good immigrants—Muscle. Put 'em through an examination of strength and endurance. Billy Bicepts, of the Rough-and-Tumble Athletic Club.[25]

The immigrant question *(Puck*, Vol. 32, 1892/93, p. 422).

CHAPTER 11

The Jew and the Irish

Of all the group relations of American Jews, it is only the relationship of Jew and Irish which shows up in humor to any great extent and is indicative of political as well as social developments. The nature of these relationships, was from the beginning, unique in that they were not an American continuation of formerly existing relations in Europe. Rather, they originated exclusively from the fact of the immigration of the two groups to America and the adjustment of both to the new continent. Caricature assails the tensions between the Jews and the Irish by depicting phases of their immigration as the source of frictions and, later by making a target of their entire mutual life relationship. While the Irishman's collisions with nearly all immigrant groups, especially with the Germans, are satirized, the Jew is humoristically described as only in collision with the Irishman. The deeper meaning of this may be that just these two groups are the ones against which the greatest objections were raised and, therefore, it was especially exciting for the humorist to bring them together. Both groups were closed in, by religion strangers to the majority of Americans and of entirely different economic stations in

166

VOL 35, NO 893   NOVEMBER 26 1898   PRICE 10 CENTS

Judge

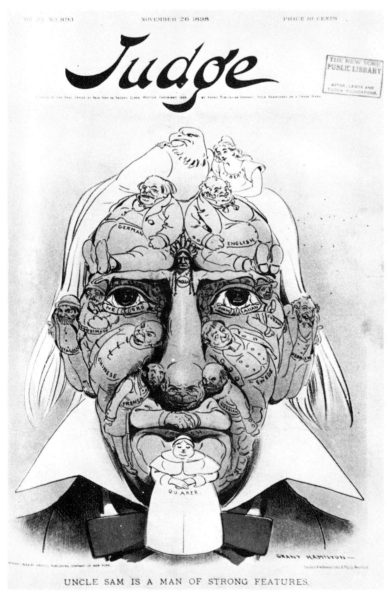

UNCLE SAM IS A MAN OF STRONG FEATURES.

Uncle Sam is a man of strong features *(Judge,* Vol. 35, 1898, No. 893, p. 1).

life. Paddy, the customer of the Jewish merchant, was either a policeman, pillar of order or, under the circumstances an unskilled worker, drinking away his wages and therefore an element of disorder. In the pictorial reports the Irishman always appears as the troublesome character among the immigrants, even in steerage on the trip and later in Uncle Sam's lodging house.[1] Moreover, the later excesses at elections, where the Irishman in the shape of a whiskey bottle fights against the German in the shape of a beer barrel, are likewise exploited. From a third side, incendiary stuff was thrown between Jew and Irishman by comparing their status at this stage since their immigration, the comparison not favoring the Irish. This setting of one group against the other was bound to heighten the tensions between the two groups.

The inciting of the two for the sake of the pleasure of laughing onlookers shows up best in a caricature of the American Congress. In it the Jews introduce the "Bill to prevent Irish Immigration" together with the corresponding "Bill to encourage Hebrew Immigration."[2] This, a commentary adds, are the Jews' plans if they could only dominate Congress.

The situation at a standstill, with continuous wrestling for primacy between the two groups, is visualized as a tug of war between Jew and Irish:

The great Finnerty-Einstein Tug of War.

Finnerty Himself: Pull, yez tarriers, pull! Be gobs, there's a nigger in the fince, av there's annything kin bate Finnerty's pull in the Twinty-nointh Warrud![3]

Actually we see in the picture a Negro helping on the Jew's side; as representative of Jewish names there already appears the name, *Einstein,* which we meet elsewhere in different situations as a symbol of the Jew's achievement in America. The collisions between the two groups are already

The Chinese must go *(Judge,* Vol. 15, 1889, pps. 58-9).

169

described early, as serious and bordering on violence and fistfights; scenes of insults are peppered with all the characteristic language of both:

> Jew: I vish you take more care vith you miserable old brick; you ash spoil mine hat a'most; why did't you shtay vere you vash, on de island in the middle of the ocean? Paddy: Bad luck to you, and more of the same; sure if it had not been for the likes of yees, ye thievin' race, the blessed Saviour would have been alive to this day, and doin' well![4]

In the collision of the two, the contrasts of their outer appearance are naturally made much of:

Accounted for.

> O'Flaherty: If it's as yez say, that the Oirish bees wan av th' Troibes av Ishrael that left the other troibes an settled in Oirland, how comes it that yez noses be so large while the Oirish have hardly any noses at all, at all? Hockenheimer: Dot vas soon egsblained. Ven your dribe left our dribes dey cut off dere noses to spite dere faces.[5]

Such a comparison of appearances, however, may work against the Jew, if, for instance, the editor is called up as an arbiter:

A lie nailed and reparation made.

> Gentleman from Chatham Street: Look a-here—, Mishter Editor, your reporter saysh I was an Irishmans. Dot's a lie!
> Cautious Editor: Certainly: it's as plain as the nose on your face![6]

Nevertheless, life creates situations where the Jew tries, with more or less chance of success, to be taken for an Irishman, so, when he dresses in a historical costume at the "hipernian masquerade ball:"

Mr. Rosenzweig: Ef dot disguises don't fool them Irish, I'll go out of der peesness. Shake Leah![7]

In the disagreeable matter of the summer resorts a saving idea may occur to the Jew standing in front of a hotel displaying a sign, "No Hebrews."

A happy thought.

Rebecca: I'll go into dot barlor and blay "Batrigk's Day" on der biano, vile you are pracing for der rooms; pe he dakes us for Irish.[8]

However, the Jewish issue in the summer resorts is mocked again by inverting the basic idea, a Jewish hotel is discovered which doesn't accept an Irishman for a guest. Its owner explains to the reporter qualities of the Irish summer guest that make him unacceptable:

The new watering place.

An event which has created some excitement in the community is the resolution of a Mr. Levi Cohen, who is the proprietor of the leading hotel at the Beach, not to admit to the privileges of his house and grounds Irishmen of any description. Mr. Cohen stated to a reporter of the New York *Season* that he did not like Irishmen on principle. They came down to his hotel in frieze coats, with shillelaghs in their hands, broke one another's heads, spilt the blood over the place much to the disgust of Mr. Cohen's German and Jewish guests, who did not at all enjoy such fun . . .[9]

An aftermath to such summer resort fantasies is to be found later even in the city:

Two Jews in a street car.—First Jew: I vill never go py Far Rockaway agen fer de summer. Nodding but Irish everywhere.
Second Jew: It's de same at Saratoga, Abey it's alive mit Irish. I vish I could go vere dere vas no Irish.

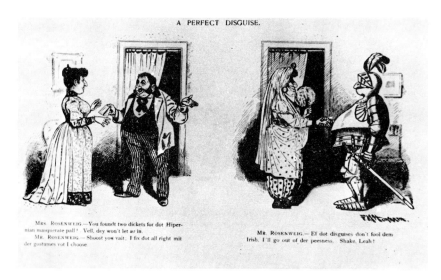

A perfect disguise *(Puck,* Vol. 32, p. 331).

Mrs. Chancey (on the opposite seat): Yez can both go to h—l, y'll find no Irish there.[10]

But St. Patrick who, according to the saying of one Irishman was a much greater man than the Fourth of July, did something for the economic relationship of the two groups on the occasion of the day celebrated in his honor:

The St. Patrick's Hat.

... The shapeless mass is quickly discovered and appropriated by the passing Italian rag-picker and within a day or two finds its way to the Hebrew hat-cobbler on the Bowery and vicinity, where it undergoes the completing process and assumes on the heads of Irish monarchs the artistic shape familiar to all who have witnessed a St. Patrick's day procession on the seventeenth of March.[11]

Less harmless in character is the meeting of the two in business. In fact, the Jew and the Irishman were not often business partners. Humorous literature has some intimations of the inexperience of the Irish in business,[12] however, peaceful cooperation between the two in one business is only possible if the expenses don't go too high:

Car fare.

An Irishman who keeps a saloon found his cash was always short, so he said to his Jew bartender one day: "Levi, did you take any money out of the register last night?"
Levi says: "Yes, I took my car fare home.
The Irishman says: "Where do you live? In San Francisco"?[13]

Fuel may accumulate against the Jew as a pawnbroker, a thoughtful shaping of the three balls, the business sign, may prevent this and at the same time conquer new territory:

How the Chinamen might "catch on" in these days
of sympathy extended to another nationality, and sneak
in with eclat.

Second-hand washing *(Judge,* Vol. 1, 1882, No. 25, p. 2).

A sixth ward Solomon.

Young Rosenstein: Vat hafe you done by the sign, Fader?
Old Rosenstein: I changed me him indo a chamrock, so
dey tink we vor Irish, and we'll get all der drade in der
district![14]

On the other hand, the Irishman's inexperience in business
is compensated by numerous inventions which spread his
fame as a trickster against the Jew. The following story of
an editor's dream moves the story of the trick played on the
Jew as far as Oregon, in itself a less probable territory, where
Jew and Irish actually meet:

Out here in Oregon, between Boise City and Happy
Camp, on the south fork of the Boise River, there is a
toll road owned and kept by a Jew, who having no charter
for his road, of course can only collect toll when travellers
please to pay it. Among the numerous teamsters who
have passed over this road was a Down Easter by the
name of Dunn, who made the common excuse, as he went
into Happy Camp with his six large freight teams that
he was *"strapped"* and promising to settle as he came
back. On coming back he found that the son of Abraham
had him charged with three hundred dollars! and, Jew
Like, remarked that that was little enough; but, said he,
"I be's liberal and I trows off half." Whereupon Jonathan
straightened himself up to the full six feet high, and said
he, "I never allow myself to be outdone in liberality, and
I'll throw off the *other half,* and we'll call it square!"[15]

As a laughing onlooker, however, the humorist appears
as if he lets Jew and Irish come to an open fight on a business
transaction. In a story, moved still farther to England, the
Irishman breaks a supposed bust of O'Connell, angered at
its poor likeness, and the Jewish seller demands indemnification. According to the Irishman's story the following
happened:

. . . when I met with that same Jew. "Want to buy, ma tear?" he ses to me, and tuk hold iv me arm. "Lave go," ses I, "ye dirty spalpeen, or it's better manners I'll be taching yer." With that . . . he begun to blarney me, and axed me to buy a figure iv Mishter O'Connell, which was as like him, he towld me, as two paes to aitch other. So I wint into the shop to have a look at it. . . . "May be," says I, "ye take me for a grane horn, but it's this I'll be telling ye, that the same is no more like Mishter O'Connell than it is like a Kilkenny tom-cat." . . . But how came you to break it; . . . It was the air in the Jew's shop turned my stomach, I'm thinking.[16]

Again, the strangeness of the Jew to the Irishman is ridiculed in the image of closed-in ethnic colonization. The Irishman, leading a hog on a rope, is ejected from the Jewish village.[17]

Where the Jew's aspirations to have a place in Gentile society is the target, his frustrated attempt is derided in a special way. The Jew, believing that he was taking one step up on the social ladder, attaches himself to another immigrant, an Irishman, and, making a trip to Ireland he learns the correct attitude toward the holy things of the Irish, which he later exploits in the conduct of his business:

Business enterprise.

To kiss me of dot Blarney stone
I vent out by Irelandt;
'Twas at der risking of mine life,
But der results vas grandt.
Dey hadt to holdt me by mine legs,
I kissed it ubside down,
'Twas by much trouble—but I was
Der happiest man in town.
It gidts me all der Irish trade;
All Baxter Street I own,
As "Der First! Original! Rosenbaum!
Vas kiss der Blarney stone!"[18]

Naturally, as in the previous tale of the Jew disguised as an Irishman, here too, his attempt at social assimilation follows the broad, basic, business theme. All categories of the personal life of a Jew are indissolubly connected with his thoughts of money.

CHAPTER 12

The Low Characters

As a mirror of the subversive social elements in America, American humor, especially in the case of caricature, is very weak. In this respect it reveals much about the hidden aggressive forces in American humor that, as low characters, it depicted nearly exclusively some Jewish underworld figures with known police records. These figures appear as one, like a superstructure, in the figure of "Marm Mandelbaum." She is described not only as a "super fence" for New York's underworld but also as the biggest headache of the police, because her case became the exemplary demonstration of police corruption. To a fighting satyric voice, the latter, and not the "super fence," is the main issue—and the Mandelbaum case is described as a catalyst. In the *Puck* cartoon, "An old saying twisted. When 'honest men' fall out, thieves have to suffer" we see the madam, the police officials arguing among themselves, and the closed store. The latter is inscribed, "Mrs. Mandelbaum Receiver of Stolen Goods." Sufficient explanations are given:

> Mother Mandelbaum seems likely to be the unconscious and involuntary instrument of much good. The fight that has arisen over that ancient mother in Israel between the

178

IT TAKES A LONG TIME TO BREAK A PET.

It takes a long time to break a pet *(Puck*, Vol. 6, 1879/80, p. 570).

Police Central Office and the District Attorney is stirring up the muddy waters of corruption, and if anybody succeeds in touching bottom, that mud-puddle may be cleared out. There is no use in speaking ill of the Hebrew race. The Jew is a valuable citizen. Even in criminal life, we see that a female "fence" of the Jewish persuasion may be a valuable factor in the work of municipal reform. Israel is not dead yet, by any means.[1]

As a final solution, not unwelcome to the New York Police, the flight of the madam became a further theme for humor. A colored caricature "Canada as mother Mandelbaum" ridicules the right of asylum granted to her there. We see in the picture a Jewish female type inscribed "Canada," leaning on the border turnpike, "Fence for American defaulters."[2]

This famous police case, which was later given serious study, hung on for a long time as a theme for humor.[3] On the lighter side, there exists, in addition, the cartoon "Scientists assert that all diseases can be prevented by inoculation," in which the likeness of the madam is drawn.[4]

As a rare example of a growing economic nightmare, depicted as the figure of a Jew from the underworld, we must examine the cartoon "The American Fagin. Instructor in the Art of stealing and getting away with it." We see in it the "Corporative Lawyer" in the figure of a Jew who teaches a juvenile "Corporation" the art of picking Uncle Sam's pocket.[5]

Some of the small police items concerning Jews appear in humor, too, as for instance, a relatively harmless infringement of the blue laws on both days of rest, Saturday and Sunday—especially in the old-clothes trade.[6] Half a century before, when the eye had only just become accustomed to the sight of the first Jew on the police force, stories of the Jewish policeman as a severe guard over the public day of rest were invented. An English traveler as far back as the years 1806–1808, recorded the following American anecdote:

Scientists assert that all diseases can be prevented by innoculation *(Puck,* Vol. 17, 1885, pps. 264-65).

A story is related of a respectable Jew at New York, who, through the malice of a powerful neighbor, was chosen constable, an office which the former endeavored in vain to be excused from serving. The first Sunday of his entering upon his office, he seated himself on a stool before his door, and every servant that went to fetch water, he took the pails from. He also interrupted, as far as was in his power, every kind of work on the *Sabbath day,* and so annoyed his enemy, and the rest of the neighbourhood with the severity of his regulations, that they were very glad to substitute another person in his place.[7]

Demonstrating unlawful behavior by using the figure of a Jew, is only of later usage, for instance in the cartoon "McKinley and the Fashions," showing "How Mr. Isaac Rosenstern and family propose to get her dresses in without payment of duties." In it we see Jewish men in women's dresses.[8] From such episodic treatment, however, grew at least one different theme, exploited rather exclusively and in all directions: the Jew's fraudulent fire insurance. Already widely used in European humor, it emerged in America suddenly, as a kind of reverse image of the fight of the American Jews against a restrictive praxis of the insurance companies, that tended to avoid the conclusion of insurance contracts with Jewish merchants by giving secret instructions to the companies' agents for this purpose.[9] Historically, therefore, the fireworks let loose in the insurance jokes, was a darkening manoeuver of prejudiced aggressive forces finding an echo in humor. The American fire insurance humor died down finally through its own exaggerated lack of reality. This happened as soon as the German Jew, the object of these jokes, had made his way as a leading, and wealthy, merchant pioneer of new commercial achievements, as for instance the department store. Finally, refusing to die, it lingered for some time as a poor space filler in humorous journals and in the joke corners of general newspapers, pointed against the Russian Jew as the German Jew's substitute. However, at the time this joke category was in full

McKinley and the fashions *(Puck,* Vol. 30, 1891/92, p. 80).

swing, its productivity was amazing. The changeover from the German to the Russian Jew as the object of the fire insurance joke expresses itself in the choice of the names that were used. The German Jew was first known as *Burn*heimer (distorting Bernheimer) and *Burn*stein (formerly Bernstein); later, fantasy names appeared: Smokenstein, Blazenheimer and Flameberg. As for the Russian Jew, his name, according to general misconceptions, had to end in ski (y); Burnup*sky* was nearly exclusively used.

A wire from the director of a New York insurance company to a branch office in Chicago, so it is told, did give instructions not to insure anyone whose name ends in —sky. In this way Mr. Burnupsky steps out, directly from the retort of namegiving into the field of caricature.[10] The legitimacy of his name is therefore proven. But also —heimers who escaped the fate of the *Burn*heimer esteem the word particle that counts:

His favorite.

Visitor: Who is your favorite poet, Mr. Ikelheimer?
Mr. Ikelheimer: Burns.[11]

The meaning and the target of the whole are clear:

No Mystery.

Isaacstein: Vot vos der cause of der fire?
Burnupsky: Der insurance.[12]

One shouldn't be diverted from the recognized target by false prophets:

At Coney Island.

Cohenstein: So you t'ink dot Gypsy vorchun-deller—vas a fake?
Isaacs: Yes; she told me dot I vould suvver a *loss* by fire.[13]

New ways to happiness make old principles appear obsolete even when they had already become proverbial:

Its origin.

Little Ikey: Who made der proverb dot three removals ish as good as a fire, Fader?
Old Swindlebaum: Some Shentile, mein sohn.[14]

Nevertheless, there are associations of thought which hold good also in new ways of life; adventurers of fantasy can walk arm in arm, as for instance Failupsky and Burnupsky:

**The glad thanksgiving of some personages
from Puck's pages.**

Mr. Burnupsky is glad that despite hard times, he has had two failures and three fires.[15]

In a borderland, business may even pair with charity:

Wanted Details.

Stranger: Will you give something for the Disabled Firemen's fund?
Burnupsky: Mit pleasure! But how vas you going to disable dem![16]

Even new insurance companies may be founded with altruistic motives:

A charity organization.

Mr. Silverbaum: Ach! doe vas goot!—anudder Hebrew charitable society shust organized!
Mrs. Silverbaum: Vot vas der name off id?
Mr. Silverbaum: Der Grabbag Fire Insurance Company off New Yorg.[17]

It goes without saying that all these principles, too, are insured only if they are handed down to the rising generation and are taken to heart by them. In the small picture "The story of a toy" we see actually the Jewish child burn the toy store given as a present to him by his father![18]

A common situation creates associations of common interest and develops an honor code for all participants:

At the Costume Ball of the Burnupsky Dry Goods Association.

Mrs. Blazenheimer: Vot vas der trubble ofer there?
Mr. Flameberg: It's dot fool feller, Smokenstein;—he was bound to come dressed as a fire—man—und dey vas pudding him oud!

In the cartoon we see only Jewish types masked in fire-red, the disguised fireman is thrown out by the other maskers.

However, the contrast between the burning dry-goods store and the asbestos store that didn't burn, may evoke laughter too, if the Jew shifts his business to the latter. Mr. "Burnstein" acts in this way:

Soldt out his glothing store and vent into der asbestos peezness.[20]

Voluntary insight may act this way, but it works as an insult if the Jew is, as they say, smoked out by an asbestos store established adjoining his own store:

"I vhas insulted to my face shust now!" exclaimed Moses, as he walked up and down in front of his clothing store in an excited manner.
"How—by whom?"
"Dis place beside me vhas for rent as you see. A stranger comes along and looks it oafer, and den, he comes oop to me und say: "Moses, vhas you insured?" 'Yes,' 'For how much?' 'Four thousand dollar.' He looks into der shtore und backs oudt again and says:
'Um! dot settles me. I rent dis place next door to keep a shtock of asbestos.' "[21]

Now, no boundary lines exist any more for fantasy. It wanders from sheer joy, recalling to memory the most elevated literary themes. Nero's view on the burning Rome, as well as the eternal purgatory are not omitted. Mere human pleasure forms only the first step for this wandering:

Pleasant recollections.

Minsky (puffing smoke in face of friend just returned from Havana): Vot does dot reminds you of, Schinsky? Schinsky: Ah! dot reminds me of dot time mein store vas burndt out. Blow me some more of dose puffs, Minsky.[22]

However, a work of art, to be really touching, must be directed to overall prevalent feelings:

The hit of the night.

Enthusiastic reception of Mr. Flameberg's tableau, "Nero Fiddling While Rome Burns," given at the annual entertainment of the Burnupsky Social Club.[23]

Finally the shadows of the netherworld are mobilized to teach Satan that even his hell fire should be covered by insurance:

At the gates of gloom.

B. Elzebub, Esq.: Well, what do you think of this for a fire?
Shade of Levinski: Grandt! Grandt! I subbose, of gourse, dot you haf efert'ing covert mit inzurance![24]

In rare cases we are allowed a peep into the evildoer's workshop:

Anticipated News.

Mr. Isaacs (in Chicago): Ish der a delegram for Mr. Isaacs sayin' dot his shtore has purned down in New York?
Hotel Telegraph Operator: No, None.
Mr. Isaacs: Vell, when von gomes shoost sendt it right up to my room, blease![25]

In other cases it is only "Happy Dreams"[26] called out by the fire, but mostly it is calculation, like any other business calculation, as in the following where Mr. Einstein functions as the calculator:

In the way of business.

What caused Einstein's fire—too much inflammable material?
No, too much insurance.[27]

Calculated in reverse—no insurance, no fire—is also sound mathematics:

A minimum Risk.

Mr. Heidleheimer: Vhat do you pay for insurance on your store?
Mr. Rosengarten: I ain'd carrying any insurance. I don't need id yed.
Mr. Heidleheimer: But subbose de blace purns ub?
Mr. Rosengarten (impatiently): Vhy how can id purn ub when dere ain'd no insurance![28]

And, even further, a fire without an insurance is sensation enough for an extra:

Startling News.

Vot's dot? Big fire at Burnupski's?
"Yes! Loss not covered by insurance! Extree!"[29]

One man's profit, however, may turn out to be the other man's loss—a loss which can nevertheless be avoided if good dreams evoke a neighborly conscience:

Cooney Dreistein: Don'd you own a lot of stock in dot North Greenwich Insurance Combany?
Mr. Schlectenheimer: Yes, vhy?
Cooney Dreistein: Den you petter sells oud. I'm insured in dot combany for dwendy dousand tollars, unt I've had a tream dot mine store purns down next veek.[30]

It is a long road from what fire catastrophe had been actually in America to what the humor magazines and newspapers made of it. Travelers in the first sixty years of the nineteenth century often report about the exceedingly frequent number of fires in American cities and farms. In New York, two fires daily could be observed. In the West, where Jews formed a considerable part of the merchant class in growing cities and mining camps, fires were even more frequent. Jewish merchants figure regularly in the list of fire losses without insurance, with extraordinary high sums lost. Frequent motives for incendiary fires were intended looting, and in rural regions, private revenge. In the cities, insurance fraud played a role. In the first incendiary trial held in New York, which was of some importance, also, for the then new branch of insurance, Jews were not among the defendants.

There is also no Jewish incendiary listed in an edition which actually represents the rogues' gallery of the New York Police.

CHAPTER 13

The Jew in German-American Humor

IT IS A UNIQUE FACT that the Germans were the only immigrant people who brought with them, on the crest of their immigration wave, larger numbers of Jews. These German Jews continued their life on the new continent in the German American cultural milieu, which later led to certain literary types of Jews in German American humor. On the whole there prevails in this humor notions brought over from the Old World, although they appear occasionally much modified by American impressions.

Running on the American track, are stories of the clothing store and the business failure like the one in

Carnival's Blossoms.

Heavenrich, Seasongood, Lion and Moses Together
Start a clothing store;
Not small like a dalfin [poorman] rather great things
And immense business is done.
Suddenly the Mischboge makes Maculle—
The creditors whisper this and that,
And search, because the result is nil,
For a bit of interest with a magnifying glass.[1]

190

A detailed, with German thoroughness systematically performed interpretation of the social obligations of the nouveaux riche is another, famous, piece of a German American humorist. He plays on American notions of Europe, corresponding to which a castle is a substitute for nobility—so sorely missed by the newly rich. Sure of the taste of his German readers, he works German Jewish gibberish into this story. The indication of American situations and of known Jewish figures in the story cannot fail to be remarked. In addition to this, the German reader enjoyed the secret knowledge of certain noble estates that Jews had acquired in Germany and, by that knowledge, compared the Jews in the Fatherland with the Jews in their new home. The highly esteemed author of this *Humoreske,* conveyed through the German American Press was Prof. Maximilian Oertel. His pseudonym was revealed only after his death when *Der deutsche Pionier,* to honor his literary creation, reprinted the whole. This gave the whole world a clear proof of what was really in the mind of an erudite German who lived together with Jews in one, democratic, society. The year of the performance of this literary deed was October 1862.[2] Therefore the whole is to be considered as a criticism of the Jews in the Civil War, with new fortunes rising among them, although the given instances are recognizable reminiscences of far older situations. The theme of "shoddy"—the word was only created during the Civil War—army uniforms produced during the war is dealt with nearly to exhaustion.

Some German immigrant circles had transferred these notions of the Jews whole, that were current in the Fatherland, often with all the prejudices intact; even bringing with them the outspokenly antisemitic pamphlet literature. They scattered the old clichés in memory of the old home or in adaptation to their new one. A few samples may be chosen here from "the sphere of the beer" in America which remained essentially German. The samples are suitable for displaying German humor also because it was just beer that made possible the founding of a great American industry that rested in the hands of Germans. In addition, it becomes clear from these pieces with what intensity the Jew was felt to constitute competition in the old world, and how this consciousness lived on in the atmosphere of German brewing in the New World.

At first it is still the merchant who is felt to be a nuisance in the brewing industry:

> Father Adam's rye—planting fed himself, his son and wife, but no money could be earned because no merchant had shown up yet—otherwise he would just have been the first Jewish businessman.[3]

But the penetration of commerce into the sacred spheres of natural work cannot be impeded, and anger is loose: "Last week a 'leather bag Jew' arrived here . . . to collect money."[4] Because beer has to be filled through leather bags, and the Jew has to furnish them, he is already in the picture "this Isaac with his signature in his face."[5] But he appears fully only when he has thrown himself on the trade with that indispensable ingredient without which beer is not beer, viz. hops. Then this Isaac may visit us "as a hop-Jew visits the country brewery, when he wants to sell as quickly as possible his dried up hops of last year"[6] by trying out all his cunning on us. The summit of shamelessness, however, is reached only in competition; for instance, if such a Jewish hops dealer would dare to found a brewery and thus call forth the German's furor, such a Jew "gives himself the designation of master brewer," but actually occupies only an "establishment of Jewish exploitation"[8] with "two shabby Jew boys." Nothing is more natural than that such a desecration of the system of German *Braugesellen* (brewing journeymen) by those who rose to become brewmasters in the new world, should enrage them to the depths of their souls and that, moreover, when such a *Braugeselle* plays a trick on the Jew, that he should

esteem its memory so highly as to relate it to future generations of German brewers. The Jew is described as follows:

> I have seen many countries, pushed on in innumerable
> breweries, only once also with a representative of the
> people of Israel who may be numbered among the most
> amusing of his tribe.
> Mr. Samuel Ketzeles was a "refined" man who had done
> business earlier, in rags, bones, and other parfumeries;
> later he became, on the ground of acquired experience,
> a hop merchant and, by his wise and cautious business
> deals, rose to be the owner of the Lerchenheimer brewery.[9]

The calming aspect of the story is that it takes place in
Europe and that, seen from an American angle, the rise of
the Jew to the station of an independent brewer is not
typical. Nevertheless, in the New World, too, something
could go wrong with brewing; some Jews, to be sure, had
made their way to brewmastering, from Alaska over the
Middle West to the East, but all in all, it was not disquieting.

Occasionally the warning voice of a truth-teller may rise
even from the beer dizziness of *"Carnevals Blüten"* and hold
a mirror before the German in America revealing his antisemitic face. The German brewer in America had forgotten
that beer was the nearly exclusive drink of German Jews in
America and had its place in all their pastimes and societal
life. At least, the truth-teller reminded them that German
theatre in America depended on Jewish sponsorship:

> Who has supported the theatre, art for a long time span.
> The favor of the mocked at Jews has liberally helped
> them.[10]

In this admonition not to forget the station of the Jew in
the German cultural life in America, nevertheless one thing
is missing: the evaluation of the Jew as the reader of the
German newspaper in America, the humorous ones did not
occupy last place.

CHAPTER 14

Observations on Jewish Caricature

AT THE END of the first decade of the twentieth century, the Jew had nearly vanished from the graphic humor of America.[1] The same may also be said of the few reminders of ethnic caricature that were left. The vanished period of the visual Jew in humor gains in cultural and historical value just through the circumstance that certain ideas about the Jew appear there in their last visual embodiments. The fact of distance, also makes it possible for us to disregard for a time at least, some of the essential ideas in these caricatures, and to concentrate, instead, on its form elements, considering subjective artistic values.

The original theme of American humor is the same as that in folklore: the animation of a landscape seemingly endless to the eye, but teeming with giant forces. This animation is brought about by the figures whose attempts to conquer nature result in adventures of all kinds. Thus, the pioneering figures in humor are the same as in the tall tale, the trapper, hunter, cowboy in their struggle with living nature; the digger and lumberman as the exploiter of timeless treasures. The farmer and the Yankee downeaster follow only in the distance, where the domination of nature already asks for a humorous mirroring of a settled rural life.

Vis-à-vis the above, the locale of the Jewish caricature is the city, with its exclusion of all scenes reverting to life in free nature, and its revelation of the inner man, projecting him to the outside. His visual motifs take the place of the preoccupation with nature; the corresponding humorous types are the urban man, with his follies, growing up to an entirely new society that completely neglected nature as its point of departure. Whenever humor still tries to use the old symbols in the new situation, as, for example, the clothier disguised as a cowboy who ropes the customer, it feels antiquated. The same may be said of comparisons of city types with wild tribes. More natural, is the struggle of humor to describe the farmer in his relationship to urban types, the first with whom he has regular contact being the peddler. The inciting of dogs against the peddler, as also any meeting of animals with city types, expresses not only the animus of the farmer, but also the symbolization of the estrangement of the city types from nature.

So much for the new things in the physical and spiritual landscape of the caricature of Jews insofar as they change the forms of graphic humor through the introduction of new subjects. The new subjective situations for the graphic humorist should also be considered in the same way. He feels, at first, that freedom of movement is restricted in the new cultural landscape of the city; the natural voices of the city don't reach him, it is only new noises on the streets he hears:

> . . . to rural persons visiting New York . . . the various cries of the city must be a source of wonder, curiosity, doubt, fear, and sundry other emotions, according to circumstances and the respective temperament of the rural persons . . .[2]

It is not by chance, but is rather deeply symbolical in meaning, that it was at that time that the first treatises on street calls were written, accompanied by humorous drawings.

Among all these types whose existence in the city is confirmed by their street cry, the Jew is already noted as early as 1866.

Street cries.

> The Polish Jew who wants to bargain with you for your cast-off hats, next contributes to the harmony of the morning with his cry. He jerks his "any old hats!" with a short stentorial chest-note, and if he happens to see you at a window, he usually gesticulates at you with a pantomime of commercial import, accompanied with grimaces that would do credit to a circus clown . . . Of all these cries none is more characteristic than that of the foreigner with the box of glass on his back, and the wooden ruler in his hand. His nasal "glass t' p't een!" resounds in every part of the city . . .[3]

Another description of the man crying out for "any old hats," gives his exterior appearance complete with trademark and stock-in-trade:

> This trader generally wears a tall, greasy stove-pipe hat, as an emblem of his vocation, and he carries battered hats of all fashions and textures in both hands, and suspended round his neck. Often he is an Irishman, not unfrequently a Polish Jew . . .[4]

"Cash for clo' pay cash clo'," was the cry of the Jewish old clo' man.

In search for the true face of this city enlivened by foreigners and, in truth, for the spiritual essence of these strangers, the quick-witted drawing humorist arrives at a new symbol, the store with used clothes (they come from old, used up Europe).

Literary protests against "old clo'" were already existent in America at a time when only England's second-hand clothing could be thought of as the agency shipping these clothes to the New World:

All the old clothes that come from England to the United States, come on the backs of the poor emigrants from the British islands.

Indignation becomes self-accusation:

If Uncle Sam has not attained that point of industrial and material prosperity which will furnish him a brand-new suit, then I have to declare—in the face of the world, and the world will agree with me—Uncle Sam is a humbug.[5]

In the revival of ancient pride in dress—, now pointed against immigrants from Eastern Europe, so much more second-hand than civilized England—we nearly fail to recognize the late renewal of primitive feelings. Nevertheless, these feelings have returned.

In "Uncle Sam's Tenement House" the new Russian Jewish immigrants sit in the apartment labeled "New York," on bags inscribed with "Old Clot . . . from Russia." When the foreigner afterwards becomes the owner of a store, this store becomes the locale where all the new observations on city life and its impulses are made. Moreover, the super-locale, the concentration of all these stores in Chatham Street, is the quintessence of it all. The fantasy of the artists as well as of the story tellers is spurred on by the

Jerusalem.—Situation south and east of the Five points, embracing Chatham and Baxter Street.[6]

The "dummies" of its clothing stores rise to become life-sized lovers and character actors in story and drawings, awakened to life and adventure by the admiring glance of a lady. Having suffered the pangs of love, they return to the store. In this style begins

Dummy and Damozel; . . .

There was no more popular Clothing store in the Bowery than that of Mr. Marmion Sholomonsh Abraham, the celebrated American tailor.[7]

A lively day in Chickentown *(Judge,* Vol. 38, 1900, pps. 104-5).

However, as soon as the first amazement and feeling of strangeness of the new subject is conquered, the graphic humorist sees the possibility of also expressing humorous situations in the images of this new milieu. In many ways the new elements of the situation appeal to the new impulses in him with which he is struggling. The trials—or more correctly the temptations—of the until then unknown, are undertaken gropingly, at first without bias or prejudice, as simple humorous drawings, effected by an acquired ability to see new things in a new light.

CHAPTER 15

Simple Humorous Drawings

THERE ARE THINGS the drawing humorist is confident of knowing so thoroughly that he doesn't consider the existence of any deviant opinion. In this category belongs his conviction of the uniqueness of the Jewish nose. This is the source of his first impression, which leads him later to become fully familiarized with a milieu otherwise so strange to him because of his birth and station in life. His security on this point is so imbedded in him that he can inscribe the drawn nose motif simply "A stinging rebuke,"[1] which means a rude refusal to all those who don't want to believe in the peculiarity of the Jewish nose. He dedicates considerable inventiveness to work out his nose as a motif in his drawings.[2] The peculiarity, he finds, is in its bigness, only to be disguised at a time when the plastic surgeon was still unknown. To cover this nose, more than a hat is necessary, as we discover from a text to one of these nose caricatures.[3] In search for its further use the caricaturist may even invent a situation where this nose represents the lesser evil. "Under Cover"[4] shows us "Mr. Nosenheimer," at the dentist, who finds that the empty space caused by pulled teeth is covered by the nose. By furnishing them Jewish noses, persons and social situations

200

Columbus Puck discovering American Humor (*Puck*, Vol. 32, 1892/93, pps. 120-21).

appear judaized and at the same time are not so strange any more to the caricaturist. Furthermore, the consciousness that "Noses and names"[5] belong together, is a lively theme.

Familiarity with individual types comes about easily, and the artist associates them with ordinary street scenes. In such scenes his humor is aroused by all the individual figures with which the street is teeming. It may be the street peddler with his tablet[6] or the "glass 't' p'teen." Added descriptions may sometimes be unfriendly, but they make clear that a simple humorous exaggeration of these types was the sole motive of the drawing. No criticism of any society was intended by it and no malice, at all. Even the Jewish clothing store may be drawn in this way.

In the demonstration of groups, be they family or purely social, much is drawn from pure observation. Street scenes like "New York's Petticoat Lane,"[7] showing the commerce on Grand Street, have no unpleasantly unnatural implications although they are exaggerated. In the imagined mass scene, "The Great American Army, as reviewed by the Potentates in Europe"[8] we see a parade of all immigrant peoples, in uniform. Among them is, also, the "U.S. Jew," treated in the same way of humorous exaggeration as all the others. Satirization of a contemporary event, in spite of a text critical of unjust behavior against Jews, may nevertheless show all the Jewish figures in caricature. This is, for instance, the case with Hilton's peace offering to Jewish charity organizations in "What are you giving us."[9] By contrast, an event sympathetic to the humorist may also bring out such caricatured figures as in "Spread of the Christian Religion. How our Hebrew friends at Tammany Hall utilize the opposition festival"[10] where Jewish women distribute presents under Christmas trees. But there is one event in the year when the Jew himself is active in American humor, "In re Purim"[11] a number of humorous drawings are handed down to us in American papers. In addition, we find the caricature of the modern Jew in a Biblical setting.[12]

Spread of the Christian Religion (*Puck*, Vol. 4, 1878/79, No. 94, p. 7).

A new field opens to the caricaturist in drawing likenesses of personalities, generally or, at least, locally known to the public. At first, the idea that among Jews there are also men who deserve to be described in this fashion had to be made acceptable. "The Gentlemen of the Jew'ry"[13] shows us five such character heads; "An evening with the great Jew—Lion"[14] who is shown as a conductor in four musical subjects, reveals that artists are also admitted among the august personalities—the adored Sarah Bernhardt figuring next.[15] Humorous papers followed her American tour at every station stop, and all her extravagances were graphically mocked. The colored cartoon in several parts, "The Bernhardt Boom in New York," shows us besides scenes of her private life also the reactions of a hysterical public to her visit.[16]

German American humor still attends on the pulse of German Jewish personalities from the old homeland. For the radical Germans, Börne and Heine are unforgettable even in America. The cartoon "Sheol"[17] shows Heine in the underworld next to Offenbach, the latter in a gastronomical mood, cutting a suckling. Heine and Börne together appear in a caricature whose text demonstrates their significance for the radicals:

> Even then there were agitators
> Agitators by right of profession,
> As one, he later showed himself to be—
> Joyfully, Mister Baruch *Börne;*
> Although he was a noble Jew,
> He agitated with insolent spirit,
> And this helped that other, on the Main
> With true flavor, *Heinrich Heine.*
> Both, with their charming writings,
> Poisoned the hearts of the people.[18]

Even occurrences among the German Jews in America, for instance a rabbinical conference with Einhorn in the foreground, may request a subject for a cartoon.[19] The Rothschild caricature is also not unknown in America.[20]

"Sheol" *(Puck,* Vol. 17, 1885, pps. 200-201).

The custom of perpetuating local personalities generally, or at least those of the same profession, in a humorous publication became fashionable at the beginning of the twentieth century. Jewish personalities are also preserved for us in this way. At that time the cartoonists themselves had already become nationally known personalities, securing with their creations the undreamed-of growth of the daily press.[21]

Peace and good will for all men *(Puck*, Vol. 17, 1885, pps. 360-61).

CHAPTER 16

Caricature As a Medium

IN OUR TIMES, the individual's feeling of discomfort and malaise in the culture of his society is recognized as the source of important psychic anomalies. The search into certain reactions to individual situations in a society that is in the past, deserves the more attention if that society is now made accessible to historical research. The North American continent, in its fast transition from agriculture to industry, from village to city, represents such a cultural psychological laboratory. There the true feelings of the individual in respect to the vast changes in the economy and in society come to a head and are expressed in an abrupt manner. An important means of expression in this process is the caricature which, although it may be wanting in some respects, appeals directly to basic human feelings. The gradations of such an appeal to feelings may have complicated variations, but, essentially, can be traced to three stages: surprise, aversion, and aggression. In the first stage, surprise, the caricaturist allows us no more than a glance into his inner mechanism, into how his reactions to new impressions, generally, come about. On the second stage of aversion, he

Puck's suggestion to the Congress of Religion (*Puck*, Vol. 24, 1888/89.

tries to shake off these impressions and this attempt, expressed in drawings, shows us the full, painful phase of confronting the new and the unexplored. Finally, in the stage of aggression, using caricature as a means of attack, we see first a wild beating about to rid himself of situations in the outside world, not of psychical ones as in aversion. Coming to its lowest level, aggression in caricature is rude primitivism, which nevertheless is soon outstripped by considerations of a rational nature. In such considerations, removal of situations are to be achieved by showing them in pictures, and caricature becomes a means of fighting. Hatred as a matter of the heart and contempt as a matter of the head, unite in caricature as a way of fighting. The antisemitic point, where there is one unclear, is only where the social situations do not show the object of the fight to be real enough. On the other hand this point is even disproportionately sharpened where social tensions around the Jew are growing. But artistic esprit is likewise a decisive factor; where real curiosity to see the new is missing, humorous ideas are also reluctant to appear. This explains the abundance of just flat and stale material in American antisemitic caricature. Many of its textual additions are simply not conceivable, unfit to create associations of thought in any greater style.

a. *Surprise and Aversion*

It exists, this strange ethnic element, and no longer does it awaken a real amazement, but it still calls forth surprise. Such a feeling is expressed by more or less jokingly made remarks about the conspicuousness of the Jew:

> "If you remarked casually that 'you saw a Jew in the Bronx today,' no one would laugh. They would say, 'Yes?' and possibly add, 'seems to me, they are getting thicker. I saw one myself yesterday, selling collar buttons on Park Row.' "[1]

At the Hockstein-Cohen Baseball Game (*Judge*, Vol. 47, 1904, No. 27, p. 16).

The place where he had been seen before only occasionally later becomes his location and is noted for that:

> This, of course, refers to the Lost Tribes of Israel and if so, we can tell Professor Wheeler an invaluable secret about them, which will greatly facilitate his labors:— They may pretty nearly all be found up in Chatham Street, near the Bowery![2]

The surprise may be the same if not the economic but the cultural station of life is concerned. For instance, if the visitor to this same Chatham Street goes to the theatre there, and expresses his thoughts about "East Side Theatricals."[3]

The new ethnic type is drawn before having landed, still on the high seas, which is in view. The caricature "Russia" shows us "Our coming Cupids. Not after Raphael, but after money."[4] First stations in economic life, may they be itinerant or settled, are shown at once in the crooked mirror. "Harvest Time"[5] depicts the Jewish street peddler swarming over the rural areas, which are characterized as, "Our peaceful rural districts as they are liable to be infested if this Russian exodus of the persecuted Hebrews continues much longer."[6] Even a forecast of the future condition of the Jewish immigrant at the level of a tramp is imagined with "A poor outlook for both."[7] The visual predictions for the "seated" trades are no more optimistic. "The shape of it"[8] shows us the figure the tailor makes, and the workman's life of "Goldstein the tailor" appears in four caricatures, "The four seasons."[9]

But the image of the peddler, forever, is the symbol of poverty, a symbol that even penetrates the political caricature. For instance, Uncle Sam is demonstrated as a tablet peddler "Forced to peddle, though he is rich."[10]

Surprise and even aversion, shown in economic life, prove, however, to be only of smaller importance vis-à-vis the same thing in cultural life. There, the Jew is destined to try many

Among the Four Hundred *(Life,* Vol. 13, 1889, pps. 334-35).

new attitudes, and aim for even higher positions, only to find them tantalizingly out of reach. Even the otherwise great equalizer—sports—takes the lead in rejecting him and in denying equality to the Jew. The overwhelming number of American sports caricatures of the Jew represents all the stages—from surprise to aggression. All these caricatures want primarily to show that, on the American sporting scene, the Jew is "entirely out of place."[11] This being "out of place" is made visual to us through types who are meant to make the drawn situation grotesque without necessarily invoking a feeling that the situation calls for a fight against the Jew. Such caricatures show "Moses on the mount"[12] and later "The owner of the winner" in "A day at the track."[13] Not less strange, the Jew appears in the riding scenes connected with hunting as, for instance, in "Mr. Diamondstein's hounds at Long Beach."[14]

The social situation, other than sports, likewise finds the Jew lacking in the social graces; in the opera box "His attention [is] distracted,"[15] and his home is inundated by snobbism. His family celebrations sparkle with extravagant luxury, as in "A brilliant wedding."[16] The "good society" of the Jews goes to summer resorts to show its wealth; so travels "Levi, Shirtmaker" to "Saratoga for the wealthy" in the cartoon "Everybody is going out of town this summer."[17] Making a show of the refined manners contracted there is a common subject. "Extenuating Circumstances" depicts this for us:

> She vas in Newport two whole days and now she can't shake off dose aristocratic airs she got dere so quick, already.[18]

All these more or less simple feelings of the onlookers at this stage are shown with more or less humor and are, by nature, more or less a prelude to openly shown aggression, which is to last for a long time.

Mr. Diamondstein's hounds at Long Branch *(Life,* Vol. 22, 1893, p. 249).

b. *Aggression.*

Aggression, in its purest form, is represented by the mocking picture. There is no plan in it and the multitude of mocking pictures of the Jew in American graphics is amazing, covering nearly every aspect of the Jew's life as an individual and as a member of a family, in economy and in society. Only his actual religious service is excepted. Since the sole purpose of these pictures is mockery, the texts often are meaningless in relation to the picture, senseless; in some cases, at best, there are half successful puns, like "A Jew de Spree" for the dandy in the picture.[19] The punster, overwhelmed by his invention, can afford to allow himself, in addition, a commentary:

> The magnificent proportion of this joke will enable the reader to overlook a peculiarity of pronunciation.

In the same category belongs a caricature "Jew Jitsu."[20] But the title may also be "Jew-Jew Paste,"[21] if, in boxing, his nose is hit. "Would improve it perhaps"[22] cuts off any thought of improving the visage of Mr. Epstein by cutting ("to cut off my nothe to shpite my fathe").[23]

Mockery hits out at the simplest life expectation of the Jew as well as at his higher hopes. The new year, to him means a little Jewish Cupid with a dollar bag "1913" and the title "A Happy New Year" in Hebrew letters.[24] His ballot, given to a candidate not pleasing to the humorist (Theodore Roosevelt) is "like voting for von off our own beeble."[25] The multitude of Jewish theatrical caricatures shows at least as many purely mocking pictures, as complaining ones.[26] The Jew's love of nature, in words and pictures, is also treated in this way. A sentimental attitude toward nature, attributed to him, follows European models of caricature:[27] Status is the only motive for cavorting in fields and under trees, and thoughts of money trouble him incessantly as, for instance, in the text of a caricature about golf:

Among the Four Hundred *(Life*, Vol. 13, 1889, pps. 258-59).

Goldstein (about to drive): . . . "Like it! I hate it! I hate
der whole beesness—golf, nature, summer, all ov ut!"
His friends: "Then vy do yer blay, Ikey?"
"Because I'm going to get my money's vorth oudt of der
glub."[28]

There is no difference in the treatment given the Jew
where the social graces are concerned.[29]

Family life and the education of his children are the two
fields where the Jew is subjected to the least tension from
the outside world. Deriding him in this respect merely as a
husband and father, without relating to his other principles
in life can therefore produce only a mocking caricature.
But these two fields are also the realms where he received
the greatest acknowledgement of the Christian world, often
applauded for his family piety and his desire to give his
children a higher education. The pertinent mocking caricature, in this case, is more a sign of the feeling of impotence
at the inability to beat him on his own (family) terms, than
a kind of deeper insight or observation of characteristic
features:

"History as it might have been. The Return of the Prodi-
gal Son"[30] shows us the lost son's return as a rich man to
"Cohnhurst Manor" and his family happiness there in strong
colors. This kind of mocking caricature reaches from the
small child and his playthings to the worries of the elderly.
Reminding him of his station in life reaches into the harmless things of his privacy: "Fish Cakes a la Financiere," reads
the bill of fare; but when Mr. Homitsky, who is in the
pawnbroking line, ordered them he had no idea how they
would be served."[31] (The caricature shows us the waiter
serving three fish balls on a fork).

The essential effect of the mocking caricature cannot be
defined easily. Often it is only a deviation of the smallest
kind from observed nature, comparable to puns in which
the change of only one letter produces an entirely new

The Horsemen of Israel *(Puck*, Vol. 6, 1879/80, p. 629).

image. The caricaturist himself characterized, for once, this procedure:

> A simple termination often changes the entire meaning of a derivative. Sheen, for instance, is a shimmering light; but a brief termination makes it an Israelite.[32]

Jewish family life and educational endeavor could easily have been drawn in light colors, but derision needs to see this all only "as it might have been."

c. *Aggression in tension and clash*

Pictures sprung to life from this psychic ground are fit to express imagined situations just as well as the reaction to real ones. To the former, belongs a group of caricatures whose originators want to show the arrival of the Jews by historically disguised mockery. "The landing at Long Branch"[33] pictures the first Jews, to whom the later aristocracy is to be traced, at the moment of their landing: "His watch and chain is still in possession of a family in the New Jerusalem, with the founder of which Columbus 'soaked it for eighteen dollars.' "

Nearer to what the eye could actually see at his time, are the visions of the caricaturist of a contemporary place. The cartoon "The New Jerusalem, former New York. A scene on Broadway in 1900"[34] fantasies a parade of a Jewish regiment over an entirely judaized Broadway, asking rhetorically:

> . . . is it too much to believe that by the time the nineteenth century has passed in its checks . . . that the "crack Seventh" and the gallant "Sixty-ninth" will be changed in name and personnel, that even our "Finest" will have given away to the aggressive Jew . . .

It is a feeling of being ill at ease in an imagined situation, that the caricature attempts to ward off.

Harmless protest is of another kind, for instance against

Bottom Facts (*Puck*, Vol. 25, 1889, p. 243).

the Christmas purchases made by Christians in Jewish stores. In "The spirit of Christmas in New York"[35] "St. Klausenstein" is shown selling toys to children.

d. *Antisemitism.*

Humoristic publications often take on an attitude to Jewish questions far outreaching any single joke or textual interpretation of an individual caricature. Insofar as even after 1870, the great mass of Jewish caricatures appeared in periodicals, we have to do with a matter of editorial policy. The humoristic newspaper justifies in its editorials, the basic tendency of a certain group of Jewish caricatures (theatre, sport, and so on). Beyond this, the paper goes so far as to publish editorially its conception of general Jewish situations and questions. Both types of editorials are highly informative on tendencies in contemporary American society in respect to the Jews. This is especially true in the case of *Life,* which bases its birthright on the claim that sophisticated society needs a sophisticated organ. Acknowledgment of this sophistication is demanded by *Life* also in respect to its expertise on the Jewish question, at least insofar as such a thing exists in America. Foreign experts may understand foreign lands, but they will learn soon, when they come to America, that this country can deliver its expert opinion without foreign help and can even give the foreigner some considerations along the way:

> It is not unlikely that Dr. Ahlwardt will find that he may derive more valuable information from his visit here than he imparts.[36]

Indeed, let's not wait too long for such valuable information!

Life continued to give summary explanations of situations involving Jews: "There is little sympathy here in America for the Jew. He has contaminated everything in American

NEWSPAPER TYPES – A STREET-CAR STUDY.

Newspaper types—a streetcar study *(Puck*, Vol. 32, 1892/93, p. 38).

life he has touched."[37] It illustrates the unsympathetic, hostile response on a tragic occasion with a picture.

Pax vobiscum.
Hard on the Jews.

The Jews of New York feel themselves aggrieved because of the failure of the Police Department to take action about the riot at Rabbi Joseph's funeral. But one thing is clear enough, and that is that the riot was highly discreditable to the police. The funeral was a demonstration without precedent, attended by enormous, unorganized crowds. The Police Department knew it was coming and ought to have made adequate preparations to take care of it. The truth was the police neglected it, and a row speedily developed into a riot, because there were not policemen enough on hand to check it on the start. The New York police force is largely Irish. The Jews say it not only fails to give them true protection, but that the members of the force habitually treat the East Side Jews with contempt and frequently with brutality.[38]

There is also not omitted from *Life*'s commentary the usual bow to the "refined Jew:"

Life has always admitted the existence of the "intelligent, intellectual and refined" Jews of whom our correspondent speaks. It sympathizes with them in their suffering from the acts of the great majority of their race. *Life* has never criticized the Jews for their religion, but for their racial characteristics.[39]

But how it presented the noble Jew to its readers may best be seen from its notices on the philanthropist Baron Hirsch: "He wished for distinguished social recognition in Europe, but that was impossible for him to buy in the measure that he desired because he was a Jew. . . . Finally he turned to charity. . . ."[40] Connecting this at the same time with Jewish immigration to America, so displeasing to *Life,* it has the following to say about the greatest philanthropist of his time:

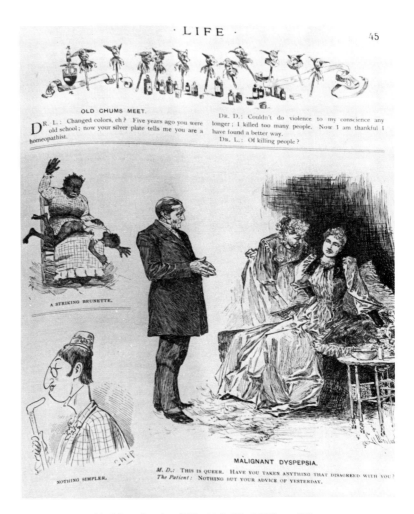

Nothing simpler *(Life*, Vol. 21, 1893, p. 45).

That eminent philanthropist, Baron Hirsch, combines with his beneficence the well-recognized shrewdness of his race. Of course it didn't take any special cleverness to find out that we inhabitants of the United States constitute the biggest fool nation on earth. But it was rather clever to pick out this country as the dumping ground for all the shiftless, incompetent, lazy, ignorant and diseased objects of his charity, whom he couldn't locate in any other country.[41]

Furthermore, it goes without saying that the Jew, however refined or philanthropical, is not clubbable because he is ready to take "club secrets outside of the club houses."[42]

We have to keep in mind that *Life* and the later *Judge* employed the most noted caricaturists of the times executing *nolens volens* their editorial policy. Furthermore, if we are clear as to the vast distribution of these publications, we cannot doubt their potential effect. *Life* is prepared to boast that it outdid, in respect to its distribution, even the yellow press, and does it with suggestions of antisemitism:

Brother Jewlitzer hasn't taken up our bet yet as to circulation.
Step up, Brother Jewlitzer, and get that D 10.000 checque —if you can.[43]

Life indulges in a mass of anecdotes, apparently for the purpose of justifying its editorial policy.[44] In one case, the subject is even a musing on Jewish names, of course as always, in the spirit of Americanism, adorned with a bet:

Editor of Life:

Will you oblige a constant reader by deciding whether "Blume," "Schuessler," and "Sweitag" are Hebrew names? This is not an idle question, but arises from the following circumstances: One day last week, the writer was going downtown on a Broadway car with a friend who is afflicted with sporting tendencies. As we passed through Union

Square he suggested a little game which should serve to pass away the tediousness of the journey. He offered to give me five dollars for every name we saw on the signs between Fourteen Street and Park Place which was not the name of a Hebrew, if, on the other hand, I could give him a dollar for every one that was. When we reached Park Place I was D 46,317 behind with D 18.00 depending on the three names. Please decide whether I owe D 46,392 or D 46,320.[45]

The *Judge* deals more summarily with the same problem. In its extensive commentary to the cartoon "The last Christian sign" it predicts the extinction of all non-Jewish names of firms. "Yes, even the familiar name of Smith and Brown may disappear from our store fronts, and those belonging to Jews usurp their place."[46]

The *Judge,* boasting in its first number of its independence from both political parties, indulged in open antisemitic attacks by means of long-winded commentaries to the cartoons of important caricaturists. In "The Jews and the Flood"[47] America is put to shame because "the hordes of them that are swarming to our shores from Russia and Poland" are helped whereas the Mississippi flood victims remain empty-handed. Even five years after the Saratoga affair appears

The Jews Revenge.[48]

. . . It seems like an idle boast when a Jew banker of national reputation said, at the time the proclamation [of the exclusion of the Jews from the Saratoga Hotel] was issued, "I will give Hilton five years to ruin A. T. Stewart a. Co.'s business and retire." The five years have not yet elapsed, and this distinguished Jew still lives, and has the proud satisfaction of seeing his prophecy fulfilled. . . .

The *Judge*'s continuous attention is directed to Russian Jewish immigration; in this matter, the paper believes that it can count on its instinctive rejection by the native American. In the following, we arrive at the *Judge*'s image of "Let my people go," demonstrated according to the example set by the Russian Jews:

A fellow Sufferer.

Poor old Pharaoh, how he has been traduced by the gospel sharps of ancient and modern times. Who can contemplate our latest arrivals from Russia and blame him or any one else for not hankering after the "chosen people?" and who can fail to admire the genius of a monarch who was able to extract honest, useful labor from such unpromising material."[49]

And the full actuality of the Biblical image is confirmed by the further statement:

They have joined the strikers, and are being supported by them in idleness, which, of course, they prefer to handling freight at seventeen cents an hour.

Even the sexual taboo otherwise existing for a news service is commented on by J. Wales' cartoon "The slaves of the Jews." This cartoon shows a women's procession parading before the Jewish clothing dealers who are "Choosing the Slaves." The reader is harangued by these incendiary words:

Go to the establishments where many girls are employed and gaze upon the Jews who engage their services. Observe with what care the scoundrels select only those of pleasing form and features. Once in their employ the girls find that they must submit to the insults or lose the opportunity to earn scanty wages. . . .[50]

It is characteristic of the ways of the antisemitic caricature that the theme of the slave market, often before used in American graphic humor, is revived in respect to the Jew, and only to him, as a sexual theme.

In contrast to antisemitic commentaries of *Life* and *Judge*, *Puck* follows a conscious liberal editorial policy, accompanying bigger cartoons with responsible statements on the Hilton affair and in the matter of the newspaper controversy on the Russian Jews. Finally, the treatment of American Jews by Russia is criticized in the following words:

> Russia is treading on the American eagle's tail. She refuses to allow American citizens who fancy Judaism as a religion any more privileges than Russian Jews—who have just none at all.[51]

CHAPTER 17

Attitudes of the
Jewish Press

ONLY FROM INDIVIDUAL VOICES of the Jewish press, and by way of deduction, may we draw conclusions as to how the Jewish public reacted to all the things that were being said or shown about the Jews in pictures in humoristic publications. Certain it is that Jewish sentiment vis-à-vis the Jewish caricature was also influenced by other things which were felt as bordering it. In this category belongs the Jewish character on the stage and the use of the designation "Jew" or "German Jew" by the general press. These minor things were sharply opposed in the Jewish press as unjust and hostile distinctions between persons. However, vis-à-vis the caricature, the recognition of its function in public life is rather broadminded. It is wholly understood that mass media of the intellect are here at play, through which the Jew satisfies his sense of humor in the same way as all the other readers. Furthermore, his showing up in caricature only confirms the significance of his life station. Even exaggerated cruelties don't awake self-pity, and criticism of excesses move rather on the rational level, finding fault with what must seem absurd to common sense. The following voice of a reader of the Jewish press may be taken as a good summary of existing sentiment and of how this sentiment was expressed in internal discussions among Jews. Finally, that all these discussions caused a desire to bring the matter before the public, likewise becomes clear:

> . . . I am sorry to say that jovial *Puck*, of New York, the little giant of caricature, has lately given us a sample of fallibility . . . we ask the talented master whether, in the cartoon illustrating the impending difficulties of the forth-coming Cleveland administration, the caricature of the Jew is in its proper place. "Auch Du, Brutus! Keppler!" Does the genius of the artist really need bygone, hack-neyed tools to sharpen his wit and humor? We indorse his right to caricature the Jew with all his racial little but glaring faults, just as he does the Irish, German and English follies. But we object to the method of making the Jew the innocent target of national dishonesty. The large business failures of this country are headed by most prominent names. Merchant princes of all nationalities have failed, and if not for "preferred creditors," these men could not continue to live in the same princely style in spite of reverses.
> Why, then, shall the Jew alone receive such undue promi-nence? Because of a small degree, and by a very limited minority, he tries to imitate his equally careful, Gentile neighbor.[1]

Real excitement, however, arose in the case where the humorist was found to be ethically deficient. Even recog-nition of all his other merits are then of no avail. The fol-lowing rejection of a mocking caricature of the Russian Jews was caused in spite of a full understanding of the function of caricature. And even under recognition of the other efforts of the paper which was found to be at fault in this case:

Shabby Knocks.

> . . . Aleck isn't sweet on the Russian Jews, and knocks quite maliciously at them whenever he gets a chance. Of course his non-Jewish readers will think it all fun to say

the meanest things about the poor refugees, but the hundreds of Jews in Texas who read the *Siftings* think quite differently. I have no wish to interfere with Aleck's fun. No one objects to his putting a second-hand clothing dealer alongside of Gus de Smith and Uncle Mose, and let the trio have a talk on Galveston or Austin Avenue. The humorist seeks for eccentricity or childlike blandness and no one needs to question his character. Joe Aby for months and months discoursed in the New Orleans *Times* —upon the famous Hoffenstein and his clerk German, and no one felt hurt, because the young humorist simply presented a character as it actually exists in the large thoroughfares of every city of the Union. Aleck Sweet has also more than once taken off a Jewish character without having given offence. But when he undertakes, in a serio-comic vein, to say ugly things of our poor Russian brethren, he creates a department which I style "shabby Knocks." I know Aleck Sweet for a just and enlightened gentleman, and I hope he will not disregard this request to leave off sneering at a class of people who suffer already more than they can bear.[2]

All in all the Jewish reader of humoristic papers took a position to Jewish caricatures there in letters to the editor. *Puck* gave in such a case

Answers for the anxious.

. . . We have never made fun of the Jews as a race or of their religion. We have made fun of the follies and absurdities of Jews, just as we have made fun of the follies of Christians and atheists and we shall continue to do so.[3]

An exemplary synthesis of a liberal policy statement and a humoristic drawing is given by *Puck* in a cartoon "The chosen people." We see there the Jewish people symbolized by a peddler whose ribbons and other notions carry inscriptions like, Sobriety, Industry, Poetry, Literature and Science. The text to the drawing says:

I have thriven on this sort of thing for eighteen centuries —Go on, gentlemen, Persecution helps de Pizness.[4]

Conclusions

THE TRANSPLANTATION of a considerable part of a Jewish generation from Western, Central, and Eastern Europe to a new soil—in its extent a first in modern Jewish history— resulted in a meeting of the Jew with an entirely new society. This meeting forms the broad background of all the literary and graphic creations treated in this study. The new society was formed by nearly all European nations, by way of emigration, among them a few the Jew had not yet met in Europe. The thinking, feeling Jew, partly developed in the spiritual sphere of the European freedom movements, is the subject, the native, or perhaps also immigrant, artist the originator of the visual inspiration deriving from the sight of the Jew. In many cases this immigrant artist was still subjected to the old European image of the Jew.

As a son of European provincial regions, hailing from most unpretentious places whose name he carries on his back as his family name, the Jew is suddenly thrown into the whirl of rising big cities. In their streets and port installations he is seen busy with the humblest occupations as well as with some more fanciful ones. His name, just as strange as all the new things around him, becomes indicative of new unfamiliar things, going hand in hand with the sound of his name. The little fellow from the smallest place in Europe is bound together with the big city more than any other immigrants. In all change-producing new situations, in all geographic movements of settlement points situated at rivers, canals, railroads, and roads he is earliest in the picture. He is it, too, in the transmigration from the small to the big city and from there to the metropolis; in this way he becomes a symbol of movement and mobility in the country.

In opposition to all this stands the artist, be he writing or drawing, in the role of an onlooker, always on an immovable point. He may be thrown into new situations by his observation, but he always needs to keep a distance to things which the Jew, being and acting in the midst of them, cannot have. Moreover, the artist always seeks a resting point, a still point, in all the changes around him, and falls back upon himself forcibly negating the compulsion to be thrown off from his preconceived image of the Jews. He tries to fortify himself by imagining his personal needs as those of all of Gentile America. However, this America could go along with the artist's imagination only in chosen moments of art consumption; otherwise it is bound to the same elements of movement as the Jew, moving ahead together with him.

The inevitability of this unacceptable situation is accountable for the cruelty of wit and, more often of caricature, which is so repulsive to the reader, and the responsible onlooker. Often this cruelty is only the self-torture of the creative mind in a world forming against all the principles of the spirit as he feels them.

This has little to do with biographical details of the jokesmiths' and caricaturists' life. The latter, in particular, immediately found the way to greener pastures when the caricature, through the technical revolution of reproduction, was able to reach the masses so much faster. At that time, the ethnic caricature had simply to give way to other more hopeful subjects of mass culture. The biggest names of

American artists were active in the aggressive Jewish caricature at least for as long as this kind of a caricature was in
vogue. Not one of them was infatuated with it, nevertheless,
Jewish caricature was not created without conviction. It
only gave way when another pattern came to the foreground.
To the extent that the new America finally succeeded in
changing the convictions of the artist, did Jewish caricature
cease coming to the fore in artistic expression.

Literary aggressive humor against the Jew had been
silenced in many cases by a changed policy of the editors of
periodicals. Cultural psychological experience, especially of
the last decades, taught us that people forced into silence are
only rarely reconciled to their fate. We may therefore look
back, somewhat relieved, to a time where literary and graphic
humor let us see the existing society in clear and historical
terms.

As a piece of cultural history the treatment of the Jew in
early American wit and graphic humor represents a sum of
emotions and ideas, even reflecting the thoughts of a contemporary collegium of literary and graphic artists. To deal
with the biographical details of these artists would, in most
cases, show no cause for the kind of treatment they meted
out to the Jews. Besides, more than in any other graphic
genre, the humorous creation is the result of the collaboration
of innumerable co-workers whose names do not show up at
all. This holds true of the drawn brain waves of the crowded
cartoon just as well as of the textual additions of the simple
drawing or caricature, be this only a title or an underlaid
joke. Murger has once pointed to the fact that in literature,
too, it is not the generals who perform the battles, but the
sergeants who train the common soldier. For literary and
graphic humor this is true to an even greater extent. In
addition, in the humoristic position of the Jew there are no
combat announcements which could be connected with certain personalities, as for instance Tweed was with the Tammany tiger of Thomas Nast. Cultural history takes a noiseless

course here, the steps of the nameless Jew (although they were furnished with humorous names) are recorded.

Just as little are we helped by *post factum* recognition of individual humorists; for instance if one of them writes: "I used to dislike the Jews cordially. But humor is a singular resolvent."[1] It is not important for our theme, but what the circumstances were in which they could become expressed in wit and humor is important.

Even occasional coworkmanship of a Jew, as the publisher of a humorous publication, represents no real paradox. An average publisher could hardly resist emanations of the general spirit of the times, the more so when they were carried on the wings of anonymity.

That the role of the Jew in humor symbolized the urbanization of America is at last a recognized *factum*. On the other hand, with some hindsight, it may be said that the first sympathetic Jewish cartoon (Harry Hershfield) originated only at a time when the urbanization of America was already accomplished. Only then could the fate of the Jewish urban go-between-of-the-occupations be felt as something common to city occupations, generally, and the humorist could reveal it. Aby, the agent's sorrows and joys did now become the experience of a city class numerous enough to include also the Jew.

The task of revealing cultural historical connections from the many seemingly unconnected ideas of the humorist is meaningful in that it helps to round out, and make three-dimensional, the picture of an era. Insofar as all this seemingly unconnected material hangs together on the Jew, it clarifies at least one cultural aspect commonly expressed by all the humorists: the difficulty of a psychically still rural America to encompass the new capitalism. This difficulty to understand, and reluctance to adapt, was alleviated by the figure of the Jew. Masson's self-recognition "There is an atmosphere, largely of cities, that can only be understood when one understands the Jewish mind"[2] explains how the humorist tries to make the situation clear for himself.

At the end of the Civil War America had only one real humorous periodical (*Mrs. Grundy*) and the Jew as a humoristic figure emerged only sporadically there. He did not then meet economy and society with the same intensity with which he assaulted them—jumping in headlong as soon as the big periodical publications with cartoons began to appear. Before this time the humorists who were recognizably known to the American public could be counted on the fingers of the hand, and they were, all in all, unimportant as critics of society. In the literary process of self-understanding and self-evaluation, American humor first met the argument that it didn't reach the full height of ethnic humor:

> It is urged as a reason against our having the humorous gift that as humor flows out of peculiarities of character and conduct, we cannot have a national humor original and unique because of our cosmopolitanism; that if we have any humor, it will so partake of the quality of every other people as to be wanting in a distinct American quality. . . . It was only the other evening that the writer addressed a meeting in New York City. It was composed of Hungarian Hebrews mostly. They drank lager, while the band played the *Mulligan Guards*. It was more the E. pluribus bragh, Erin go unum!

But this opinion was to be disproven; in fact, exactly the opposite took place:

> From the commingling of heterogeneous customs and languages we shall have a medley full of fun, loud, large, uproarious, and rollicking in exaggerations.[3]

Consequently, where uniqueness is claimed for American humor, this quality can be traced back exclusively to the cosmopolitan character of its population.[4]

Actually, the world did not expect American humor to be a mirror of ethnic groups. What it wanted was rather to see the shocking and the previously unheard-of, every newly rising social and cultural craze, and the many extravagances of individuals. Social criticism expressed in humor was overlooked, and even the changing economic situation in an urbanizing America—basic for the role of the Jew in American humor—was not noticed or paid any attention. Its far-reaching independence from European subject matter in wit and in literary figures of farce and clowning endures after all. The same may be said of the early transplantings of the European humoristic anecdote, which soon perished in its new surroundings not having the advantage of novelty. Eruptive in its basic character, American humor does not cling for long to the remembrance of things which are no longer new. A rude compromise with old things is made only in its pictorial humor, where it has to come through with situations that are already rooted in the consciousness of the masses.

A comparison of the European Jewish caricature with caricature in America, allows us to make some final conclusions. In American caricature the Jew is a reasoning being, laughable in his weaknesses, but formidable in what has to be—however unwillingly—recognized as his strength, rationality above all. In European caricature the Jew remained the devil—effecting the fastest transition in the world, from good to bad—and, therefore, fathering all evil in society including social tension. In Europe, he was mocked, reviled, and cursed, never really laughed off. American caricature exposed forces and situations of the inner man; the Jew, by his reasoning, evokes the criticism of society; but this criticism was also a result of the self-criticism of Gentile, artist, and public. In Europe, the symbol of the Golden Calf led to Jew-baiting and pogrom; in America, to a wrestling with spiritual forces which, in time, and after two millenia of antisemitism in Europe, made possible an equilibrium of social forces in a new world.

Appendix

Anecdote and Humorous Story

I<small>N THE EARLY PERIOD</small> of the American anecdote and full-fledged humorous story, the narrator was without name or recognizable shape. It took a longer time before there arose, from among the staggering number of figures who enlivened the frontier experience of the new America, firm figures. Moreover, figures of such a character, that importance, and even wisdom, could be attributed to their experiences to be handed down to other people.

The basic American character was pragmatic, not easily accessible to fixed articles of wisdom. Americans were also not furnished with centuries-old experiences which formed the wisdom rules of the European proverb. Therefore, the essence of American life experience is crystallized mainly in the narration of occurrences from which practical wisdom could be derived. In its beginning, this story, short anecdote, or didactic longer tale, was not yet embellished with humoristic features, and the person of the narrator was without any great interest, and so better left without a name. Later, when something like a folk hero or an imagined democratic folk figure (or even an acknowledged wisecrack) had arisen, freely invented stories were told in his name. This design was later followed by all the humorous organs and humor sections of general newspapers. "Editor's Table" reveals how the writing newspaperman takes down the words of figures whom the reader, himself, may have met in life and suggested. This may be a sailor, a soldier, or a storekeeper, a dissatisfied customer or even only a tramp; the real narrator, however, now has taken shape.

Early American jest books are still very much dependent on European material and also use Jewish stories from the Old World (1796):

> A wealthy Jew, who was tired of living in Berlin, and had made frequent applications for leave to quit that place, which he dared not otherwise attempt, at last sent a letter to the king imploring permission to travel for the benefit of his health. The king immediately sent him the following answer, written with his own hand:
> Dear Ephraim,
> Nothing but death shall part us.
> Frederic.[1]

Other early anecdotes may be credited to the impact of the Bible people on the spiritual world:

Humorous anecdote.

> A number of students happening one evening at an inn, the conversation. . . . "What if he know the scripchure, and understand all the mysteries of the Jewish ritchual?—I say, of what service is all this to a man, while his heart is hard to the poor?"[2]

Such a student appears also as the person of whom familiarity with the strange Bible language may be expected, and he may be rightly referred to this language if his speech is improper:

> A lady riding in a car on the New York Central Railroad was disturbed in her reading by the conversation of two

young men occupying the seat before her. One of them
seemed to be a student of some college on his way home
for a vacation. He used much profane language greatly
to the annoyance of the lady. She thought she would
rebuke him and begging pardon for interrupting them,
asked the young student if he had studied the languages.
"Yes, madame, I have mastered the languages quite well."
"Do you read and speak Hebrew?" "Quite fluently."
". . . Will you be so kind as to do your swearing in
Hebrew?"[3]

It didn't take long before an American Jew showed up
as a dispenser of wisdom, and an anecdote was told in his
name. Characteristically, this concerns a person who had
already tried a venture in the realm of politics and had
accepted a public office:

Jeu d'Esprit.

When the late Mr. Noah, who was a Jew, was a candidate
for the office of sheriff of the City of New York, an objec-
tion to his election was that a Jew would thus come to
have the hanging of Christians. "Pretty Christians,
indeed," replied Noah, "to need hanging."[4]

As a direct reporter to the newspaper editor, delivering
humorous stuff to him, the Jew does not appear very often.
The following piece, mixing together all kinds of possible
information, is remarkable because it hails from the South
during the Civil War and gives us clues to the behavior and
perception of the soldiers:

A Jewish reader of the Drawer, who sells jewelry, writes
to us:
Some of the soldiers in and about Memphis have been
rather taken in by some of the not over-scrupulous store-
keepers in that city, and, as a necessary conclusion, have
set the majority of them down as a parcel of swindling
Jews. Some of them, however, have rather mixed emotions
as to what sort of a being constitutes a Jew. I keep a
jewelry store in Memphis, and have much dealing with

soldiers. Few of those I have come in contact with have ever discovered the fact of my being a Jew. A captain who pretends to have great faith in me came to my store some time ago, and begged me to go with him and look at a certain golden chain which he wanted to purchase, and which the little "Irish Jew" around the corner kept for sale. "You know," said he, "I can't believe what this Irish Jew tells me and wish you would go with me and look at the chain whether it is good gold or not." The idea of mistaking poor Paddy—who, to my certain knowledge, goes to the "praste" as regularly as he goes to his meals— for a Jew, and then the above request, had something so ridiculous in it, that I experienced hard work in keeping my risibles down. I told my friend the captain, however, that he was quite right—that Irish Jews were least of any trusted. I went with him, looked at the chain, and on my recommendation he purchased it.

A *chaplain* of an Illinois regiment, in speaking to me of *two brothers,* remarked that one of them was a Jew, and a mean man; and "the other not a Jew and a perfect gentleman!" Some soldiers congregated in my store the other day, got to speaking as the best way of discovering whether a man was a Jew or not. One of them stoutly asserted that every Dutchman was a Jew. Others made observations equally wise. But one of them finally capped the climax by asserting that every man who fell on the original price he asked for an article was a Jew![5]

In most of all the anecdotes having to do with the Jew, however, he appears only as the subject about which something is told. As a speaker he is recognizable only by occasional phrases or by imitations of his speech. His personality appears just as obliquely and is properly unlocked only by the peculiar features given to him in the anecdote. In most cases he merits no further physical description if we don't take the stereotype "little" as such. An anecdotal Jew with an effective personality who appears in America is only the European, Rothschild; of him every personal detail merited anecdotal treatment. His stature in the Old World can be measured by comparison with other figures of the

Old World; in the end, however, the anecdote reaches back to his Hebrew heritage:

Facetiae.

Baron Rothschild and the Archbishop of Paris chanced to dine together one day at the house of the Duchess A—. The Jewish Baron insisted that the Catholic Archbishop should take precedence, while the prelate wished to set an example of tolerance by his finished politeness. As both civilly insisted, the Archbishop suddenly exclaimed: Baron, you are the son of Moses, and I am the servant of Jesus Christ. You have precedence by virtue of seniority. The old Testament is older than the New. The Baron bowed and led the way.[6]

His human features are, preferably, dressed up in a grotesque manner, underlining the contrast between rich and poor:

Baron James De Rothschild, visiting Ary Scheffer's studio, found the eminent artist in a towering rage. A model, a Jewish beggar, had failed to keep his appointment, and the artist who felt in the best mood for painting, was of necessity idle. The baron gaily exclaimed: "Let me supply my absent brother's place."[7]

In contrast to the great baron the nameless European Jew is put down in his meeting with great people:

Once, said Coleridge, I sat in a coach opposite a Jew—a symbol of old clothes bags—an Isaiah of Hollywell-street. He would close the window; I opened it. He closed it again; upon which, in a very solemn tone, I said to him, "Son of Abraham, thou smellest! son of Isaac, thou art offensive! son of Jacob, thou smellest foully! See the man in the moon! he is holding his nose at thee at that distance. Dost thou think, that I, sitting here, can endure it any longer?" My Jew was astonished, opened the window forthwith himself and said he was sorry he did not know before that I was so great a gentleman.[8]

In the New World even the nameless Jew may be rather ebullient and is occasionally permitted to render a bon mot:

> Among the men who served among Roosevelt's Rough Riders in Cuba was a little Dutch Jew, who, according to the men in his own troop, was "the very incarnation of cool imprudent bravado in a fight." He was a consistent fatalist. One day he observed a comrade dodging a spent bullet that had whistled uncomfortably close to him. "Vat's de use to todge dem pullets?" sang out the little Jew. "Dey'll hit you shust as vell vere you are as vere you ain't!"[9]

A tale in reverse of the "little Jew," name dropping, is put in his place in the following story (1855):

> Quite an amusing hoax has just been played on some of the passengers. There is a very talkative little English Jew merchant on board who got bruited around as being the Lieutenant Governor of Jamaica. Having made himself disagreeable to a party of gentlemen, they were disposed to "snub him," but on learning that he was a high functionary of Jamaica, one of them, Judge McAlister, of the United States District Court of California, proposed making amends by treating him with more civility and attention. He accordingly gave him a special invitation to drink wine with him. Some of the party expressed to the Judge their incredulity of the man's holding any high official station. But he insisted that there could be no mistake about it, as Captain McKinstry had assured him of its truth. Seeing the Judge, shortly after his tête-a-tête with the Governor, we asked him how he fared with his excellency. He replied with much irritation—"The fellow is a contemptible humbug."[10]

Lining up against the Jew may create solidarity among people who, in other respects, stand on different sides of the barricade. The following anecdote from the Civil War shows us the Union soldier-prisoner, following the inclination of his heart, making common cause with the Confederate prison guard:

Once upon a time, at a place and date which had maybe
better not be given, a gang of Confederate cavalrymen, of
that class which . . . we call bummers, boarded a railroad
train. . . . There were a number of Jews on the train, *en
route* from the more southern city to buy goods in the
other and more favorably located point, and their pocket-
books were well lined. The bummers were prancing around
in this crowd and going through the sorrowful Hebrews in
a scandalous way, when, it is related, a . . . Michigan
cavalryman . . . said . . . You see that Jew sitting over
thar. I see him taking his pocket-book just now, and
stuffing it under the seat. I wanted to give you the pint.
I don't want to be misunderstood. . . . You needn't think
that I'm trying to curry favor with you fellows, becuz I'm
a prisoner. I've fit you for three years and I'm goin' at it
agin as soon as I'm exchanged, but for all that, *I don't
want to see no d - - - d Jew defraud a soldier*.[11]

The story of the tricked Jew takes on life by its moving
appeal to Gentile solidarity. It uses the most diverse subject
matter taken from the stations of the Jew in life. In the
following tale the tension is heightened by the fact that
their solidarity is opposed by the solidarity of an imagined
Jewish crowd. This crowd, however, is playfully dispersed by
the intervention of natural powers. The old European theme,
Jew and dog, widely used there in literature, takes a new
American turn with the dog now appearing in Chatham
Street.

. . . there came flocking in from the back room and
through doors in the wall at either side (two or three of
these shops are strongly suspected of being confederated
in this way for the common interest), a swarm of young
and old Jews, who fastened with one mind and all hands
on the blue coat.
General Taylor, meanwhile, fretting by the counter, was
rapidly rallying all his forces for a demonstration. The
Jews were grinning with their triumph, and spitting
defiance over the counter at the b'hoy, when he shouted,
or rather bellowed, in a low grumbling tone, looking at

the dog, "Go in!" General Taylor, of whom (laying low) they hadn't the slightest suspicion, had no sooner showed his nose and his unquestionable teeth in the spring he made for the whole crowd at once, than they dropped the coat, and, huddling one a-top of the other, disappeared with lightning speed through the various ways of exit, leaving a clear field.[12]

The humorous effect may even be heightened when the Jew is even tricked by the darkie, a figure, in reality otherwise so dependent on him in economic respects. The laughing onlooker himself feels that he has long since passed the economic situation dealt with in the story. The tone of the tale is therefore not only moralizing but also condescending, in this way fortifying the total effect:

I was walking down the Levee some days ago with a young "colored gemman," intending to send him somewhere with some articles I was about to purchase. All along the Levee there are a great number of small retail, or to use the local phrase, "picayune," stores, kept mainly by Israelites. These gentlemen have a disagreeable habit of stopping the passers-by and requesting them to bestow their patronage upon them. My darkie was politely stopped by one of them, as usual, and asked if he wouldn't have a hat, or a pair of boots, or "something of the kind."
"Well," says Tom, "I believe I'll take a hat. I want one anyhow, an' I mout as well git one here as any whar."
The hats were all tied upon a string and hung down from a nail in the wall. The store-keeper whips out his knife, cuts off one of the hats, wraps it up in a piece of paper, and hands it to Tom with a profound bow and a satisfied grin. "Dollar an' 'alf," says he.
"T'ankee," says Tom, putting the hat very coolly under his arm, and walking off with it.
"Eh! where my dollar an' 'alf? you blasted nigger!" cries Moses, pouncing upon the hat.
"Debill!" says Tom; did ye *never* see sich a feller! Ax me if I take a hat, and when I say yes, and take de hat, and say T'ankee, he jump 'pon me an' want his dollar an' 'alf! Hat no 'count no how; I'd a throwed it away any how;

but did you d'ever *see* sich a feller?"—and off he walked, apparently in a great huff, but secretly dying to get somewhere where he might roar at pleasure.

The Israelite, however, appeared a *little* out of temper. The breeze, laden with sugar and molasses, received an additional load as it passed by him, which just dropped off as it passed by me, and which musn't be repeated to ears polite.[13]

To trick the Jew *in corpore,* by tricking his community, establishes a further point of attraction for the imagination:

A gentleman owned four lots adjoining a Jewish burying ground, in the upper part of the city. The owners of the cemetery wanted to purchase these lots, but as the price they offered was no equivalent for their value, the gentleman refused to accept it. At last the Jews' trustees hit upon what they considered a master-stroke of policy, and meeting Mr. V— a few days afterward, said: "Ah, Sir, we tink, you will not get anybody now to live on your property up dere. We have buyed lots on the odder side, and behint it, and it is a Jews' burying ground all around it." "Very well," replied Mr. V—, "I shall begin to build to-morrow." "Build," echoed the trustees, taken aback by the cool manner in which this was said, "why now," with a cunning smile, "what *can* you put up dere, mit a Jews' burying ground all around?" *"A surgeons' hall,"* said Mr. V—. "You have made my property the most eligible in the city. Good morning!" The reader may imagine that Mr. V— received his own price for the lots, which were speedily converted into a Golgotha, and the principal trustee now lies buried in the midst of them, with a white marble monument pertruding out of his bosom, large enough to make a resurrection-man commit suicide.[14]

Also, when the shoe is on the other foot, the tricks of the Jew are described, there is no end to the new things he invents. The following story intends to show how he goes with the times in all things financial:

A Hebrew gentleman had a legacy left to him, but it was hampered with an unfortunate condition, which he hastened to announce to a sympathizing friend. The sum was D10.000, but half the sum, according to the testator's wishes, was to be placed in his coffin and buried with him. Was there ever such a waste of good money? But the sympathizer was equal to the occasion. "Where is the money now?" and was told, "In the bank." "All right," he said: you write a check for D5000 and put it in the old boy's coffin, *drawn to order.*" That young man ought to get on in the world.[15]

The indelible character of the baptized Jew, even in the highest rank of religious acceptance, is stressed in an anecdote of North American provenance told of a former rabbi turned bishop:

The Bishop of Huron, Western Canada, is a convert from Judaism. He was waited upon recently at the episcopal residence by a Jew who buys discarded clothes. The bishop offered him a number of articles he was willing to sell, but asked such prices that the buyer and he could not trade. After fruitless efforts to beat down the bishop's figures, the peddler exclaimed, "You may be a good Christian bishop, but ven you talk old clo' you are still a Jew."[16]

Notes

NOTE FOR CHAPTER 1

1. John Orville Taylor, *Satirical Hits on the People's Education,* New York: 1839, Introduction.

NOTES FOR CHAPTER 2

1. [Holley,] *My Opinions,* Hartford: 1874, p. 178.

2. *Ibid.,* p. 179.

3. [Freeman Hunt,] *American Anecdotes . . .,* Boston: 1830, vol. 2, p. 182.

4. *Harper's Weekly,* vol. 20 (1876), p. 931.

5. *Yankee Notions,* vol. 8 (1859), p. 370.

6. "History of the American Flag," *The Spirit of the Times,* vol. 23 (1853/54), p. 268.

7. *Ibid.,* vol. 19 (1849/50), p. 416.

8. W. K. Northall, "A Learned Society," *Life and Recollections of Yankee Hill . . .,* New York: 1850, p. 127.

9. *Haney's Journal . . .,* New York, vol. 3 (1870), p. 7.

10. J. W. Wakeley, *The American Temperance Cyclopedia,* New York: 1875, p. 198.

11. "Greeley Among the Artists," *The Nation,* vol. 15 (VII–XII, 1872), p. 311.

12. Eduard Fuchs, *Die Juden in der Karikatur,* München: [1921], p. 176.

13. The often-drawn marital bed of Brigham Young is free from any Biblical intimations.

14. In that case, respect for the Bible acted against nascent antisemitism, at the price of the good laugh the American people could have had from it.

NOTES FOR CHAPTER 3

1. *Continental Monthly,* New York, vol. 3 (I–VI, 1863), pp. 237–247. In a very old version of the jest, as the result of a fraud in a barber shop, the Jew loses the money loaned to a nobleman. "Barba deceptus Judaeus." The scene of the story is Frankfurt.
2. *The Constellation,* vol. 2 (1830/31), p. 215.
3. *Harper's Magazine,* vol. 43 (1871/72), p. 4, sgd. Wm. Allen Butler.
4. Rudolf Glanz, "The Rothschild Legend in America," *Jewish Social Studies,* vol. 19 (1957), pp. 3–28.
5. According to Cecil Roth, money-lending as a Jewish occupation was more characteristic of Northern Europe, during Shakespeare's time, than Venice.
6. "The Snoblace Ball," *The Spectator,* New York: 1845, p. 58.

NOTES FOR CHAPTER 4

1. *The Laughing Philosopher,* Philadelphia: 1850, p. 12.
2. *Elton's Comic All-My-Nack,* 1834. p. 125.
3. *Puck,* vol. 44 (1898/99), No. 1127, p. 6.
4. "True Happiness," in *Puck,* vol. 44 (1898/99), No. 1121, p. 12.
5. *Scrapbook of Caricatures,* I. Halpin, New York: 18-? (New York Public Library).
6. *A Collection of Songs Selected from the Works of Mr. Dibdin,* Philadelphia: 1799, p. 260.
7. *Puck,* vol. 2 (1877/78), No. 50, p. 1.
8. *Puck,* vol. 5 (1880/81), p. 215. Help for Archbishop Purcell.
   . . . Spokesman of Syndicate: Why d'ye bodder yer brainsh, my tears? Ven yer gives us a nice little morgige on dot Catedral, Bruder Purcell shall hafe all der manish he vants. Only small percentage a veek—vell, den a mant shelp me Moses!
9. Wakeley, Ebenezer, *The Gentile Ass and the Judaen Establishment,* Chicago: 1895. The caricature opposite the title page is inscribed: The "Gentile Ass" reaches the end of his "Weary Journey." It shows the Jew as the receiver of the load; the bags are inscribed "Art," "Discoveries," "Science," "Earning."
10. *Collection of Songs, op. cit.,* p. 294.
11. "At the Pawnbrokers' Ball," in *Puck,* vol. 62 (1908), No. 1600, p. 5.
12. *Puck,* vol. 6 (1881/82), pp. 508–09.
13. *Puck,* vol. 35 (1894/95), p. 96.

14. "Dramatic," in *Life*, vol. 13 (I–VI 1889), p. 344.

15. *Puck*, vol. 27 (1890), p. 170.

16. *Puck*, vol. 17 (1884/85), p. 356.

17. *Puck*, vol. 9 (1881), p. 367.

18. "The Religious Vanity Fair," in *Puck*, vol. 6 (1879/80), pp. 526–27.

19. "The Codfish Exodus to Europe," in *Puck*, vol. 6 (1879/80), p. 178.

20. "Consistency," in *Puck*, vol. 35 (1894), p. 357.

21. *Puck*, vol. 10 (1881/82), p. 134. The firm is Isaac a. Co.

22. *Puck*, vol. 37 (1895), p. 86.

23. *Drummers' Yarns*, 2. Crop, New York: 1895, p. 69.

24. Wallace Irvin, *At the Sign of the Dollar*, New York: 1905, p. 94. *Life*, vol. 25 (1895), p. 239.

25. *Puck*, vol. 40 (1896/97), No. 1037, p. 10.

26. "Vulgar display," in *Puck*, vol. 35 (1894/95), p. 3.

27. "Instructive exercise," *Puck*, vol. 38 (1895/96), p. 98.

28. Rudolf Glanz, "Jewish Names in American Humor," *For Max Weinreich*, The Hague: 1964, pp. 63–71.

29. "Humor of the old Southwest," in Walter Blair, *Native American Humor*, New York: 1937, p. 386.

30. Blair, "The Humor of the Farmer's Almanac (1809–1836)," p. 200.

31. *Puck*, vol. 27 (1890), p. 418.

32. *New Orleans Daily Picayune*, Nov. 7, 1855, p. 1.

33. *Puck*, vol. 42 (1897/98), No. 1074, p. 16.

34. *Life*, vol. 24 (1894), p. 35.

35. Sketches from "Texas Siftings" by Sweet and Knocks, New York: 1882, p. 211.

36. *Puck*, vol. 46 (1899/1900), No. 1193, p. 5.

37. *Puck*, vol. 41 (1897), No. 1064, p. 3.

NOTES FOR CHAPTER 5

1. "American Humor and Humorists," in *The Round Table*, vol. 2 (1864/65), p. 2.

2. Grand Meeting of the "Swell Mob Protection Society," in *The Spirit of the Times*, vol. 14 (1844/45), p. 437.

3. *Puck*, vol. 14 (1882/83), p. 183.

4. *Puck*, vol. 45 (1899), No. 1152, p. 4.

5. *Puck*, vol. 43 (1898), No. 1116, p. 11.

6. *Puck*, vol. 44 (1898/99), No. 1135, p. 6.

7. *Puck*, vol. 46 (1899/1900), No. 1178, p. 5.

8. *Puck*, vol. 39 (1896), No. 996, p. 3.

9. *Tid-Bits*, vol. 1, New York 1884/85, p. 8.

10. "Baseball," in *Puck Library 1887*, No. 1, pp. 6, 7.

11. *Puck*, vol. 46 (1899/1900), No. 1186, p. 14.

12. *Yankee Notions*, vol. 13 (1864), p. 136.

13. *Puck,* vol. 46 (1899/1900), No. 1191, p. 14.

14. *Puck,* vol. 30 (1891/92), p. 406.

15. *Puck,* vol. 51 (1902), No. 1311, p. 6.

16. *Puck,* vol. 30 (1891/92), p. 326.

17. *Puck,* vol. 35 (1894), p. 380.

18. *Puck,* vol. 27 (1890), p. 263.

19. Rudolf Glanz, *German Jewish Names in America, Jewish Social Studies,* vol. 23 (1961), pp. 143–169. "Jewish Humoristic Names in America," in *For Max Weinreich,* The Hague: 1964, pp. 63–71.

20. *Puck,* vol. 65 (1909), No. 1630, p. 12; *Puck,* vol. 52 (1902/3), No. 1329, p. 3.

21. *Life,* vol. 25 (1895), p. 380.

22. Henry Morford, *Sprees and Splashes,* New York: 1863, p. 214.

23. Sinai a. Olympus, New York: 1899, p. 41.

24. *Puck,* vol. 33 (1893), p. 114.

25. *The Judge,* vol. 2 (1882), No. 30, p. 5.

26. *Puck,* vol. 41 (1897), No. 1900, p. 11.

27. *Puck,* vol. 26 (1889/1890), p. 220.

28. *Puck,* vol. 28 (1890/91), p. 327.

29. *Puck,* vol. 27 (1890), p. 135.

30. "Editor's Drawer," in *Harper's Magazine,* vol. 32, p. 134.

31. *Puck,* vol. 30 (1891/92), p. 275.

32. *Harper's Weekly,* vol. 8 (1864), p. 659. The story exists also in a rhymed form.

33. *The Barber's Shop* [1808], p. 28.

34. *Random Recollections of Albany, from 1800 to 1808,* Albany: 1850, p. 50.

35. [Locke] "Swinging round the Circle," Boston: 1867, p. 55.

36. *Yankee Notions,* vol. 8 (1859), p. 54.

37. W. H. Bell, *The Quiddities of an Alaskan Trip,* Portland, Oregon: 1873, p. 7.

38. [Mortimer Thomson] *Doesticks Letters,* Philadelphia: 1855, p. 141.

39. Charles Cist, *Sketches and Statistics of Cincinnati in 1851,* Cincinnati: 1851, p. 184.

40. *Comic Annual* (H. P. Finn), 1831: p. 192.

41. *"Shylock,"* a burlesque, as performed by *Griffin a. Christy's minstrels . . .,* New York [1876]; *Lantern,* New York: 1852, p. 173.

42. *Puck,* vol. 25 (1889), p. 70; *Puck,* vol. 9 (1881), p. 60; *Puck,* vol. 26 (1889/1890), p. 182.

43. *Puck,* vol. 28 (1890/91), p. 432.

44. *The Spirit of the Times,* vol. 14 (1844/45), p. 544.

45. "Editor's Table," in *The Knickerbocker,* vol. 42 (I–VI 1853), p. 202.

46. "Editor's Drawer," *Harper's Magazine,* vol. 32, p. 401.

47. *Sacramento Transcript,* vol. 2, No. 115 (March 10th 1851), p. 2.

48. *Puck,* vol. 25 (1889), p. 276.

49. *Puck,* vol. 39 (1896), No. 995, p. 5.

50. *Puck,* vol. 14 (1883/84), p. 186.

51. Frederic Van Wyck, *Recollections of an old New Yorker,* [1932], p. 44.

52. *Puck,* vol. 45 (1899), No. 1153, p. 16; *The Judge,* vol. 2 (1882), No. 48, pp. 8–9.

53. *Puck,* vol. 29 (1891), p. 362.

NOTES FOR CHAPTER 6

1. According to Eduard Fuchs the medieval *Judenschwein* is one of the oldest German caricatures. Eduard Fuchs, *Die Juden in der Karikatur,* München: 1921, pp. 114–123.

2. "Pork-hater," in *The Jew in the Old American Folklore,* New York: 1961, Chapter 6. Rudolf Glanz.

3. [E. G. Paige] *Dow's Patent Sermons,* Philadelphia: 1857, IV, p. 282.

4. William Kelly, *Across the Rocky Mountains,* London: 1852, vol. 1, p. 46.

5. *Mrs. Grundy,* vol. 1 (1865), p. 34.

6. [Derby, George] *Phoeniciana . . .,* New York: 1856, p. 165.

7. "Facetiae," in *Harper's Bazaar,* vol. 6 (1873), p. 480.

8. "Bribery of Conscience," in *The Constellation,* vol. 4 (1832/33), p. 284.

9. "The Food We Eat," in *Dissertations by Mr. Dooley,* New York: 1906, p. 247.

10. *John Donkey,* vol. 1 (1848), p. 335.

11. *Ibid.,* p. 323.

12. *Yankee Notions,* vol. 8 (1859), p. 370.

13. "Nose-ology," in *Oregon Spectator,* vol. 2 (1847), No. 7, p. 1.

14. *Momus at home,* Ithaca: 1842, p. 30.

15. *Flowers of Wit,* Baltimore: 1832, p. 62; and *The Humorist,* Baltimore: 1829, p. 112.

16. *A little Bit of a Tid-Re-l; or a Chorus of the Times,* by Roderick Rundelay, New York: 1824, p. 104.

17. *Puck,* vol. 14 (1883/84), p. 391.

18. *Yankee Notions,* vol. 10 (1861), p. 356.

19. *Puck,* vol. 49 (1901), No. 1253, p. 10.

20. *Puck,* vol. 25 (1889), p. 295.

21. *Puck,* vol. 7 (1880), p. 242.

22. *Figaro,* Chicago, vol. 2 (1890/91), p. 276.

23. *Puck,* vol. 29 (1891), p. 362.

24. *Puck,* vol. 48 (1900/01), No. 1235, p. 14.

25. *Puck,* vol. 7 (1880), p. 221.

26. *Puck,* vol. 7 (1880), p. 344.

27. *Puck,* vol. 7 (1880), p. 242.

28. *Puck,* vol. 5 (1879), pp. 327–28.

29. *Puck,* vol. 5 (1879), p. 331.

30. *Puck,* vol. 9 (1881), p. 118.

31. *Puck,* vol. 29 (1891), p. 291.

32. "Alas, poor Hilton!" in *Puck,* vol. 4 (1878/79), No. 94, p. 2.

33. *Puck,* vol. 5 (1879), p. 322.

34. *Puck,* vol. 5 (1879), p. 331.

35. *Puck,* vol. 5 (1879), p. 338, cartoon pp. 345–46.

36. *Ibid.*

37. *Puck,* vol. 7 (1880), p. 452.

38. *Puck,* vol. 24 (1888/89), p. 23.

39. *Puck,* vol. 36 (1894/95), p. 115.

40. *Puck on Wheels,* New York: 1880, "Dictionary," p. 18.

41. *The American Tour of Messrs. Brown, Jones and Robinson,* by Toby, New York: 1872, p. 13.

42. "Recollections of Hudson," in *Random Collections of Albany, from 1800 to 1808,* Albany: 1850, p. 58.

43. Boddam-Whetham, *Western Wanderings . . .,* London: 1874, p. 29.

44. [Locke] "Swinging round the Circle . . .," Boston: 1867, pp. 10, 28.

45. "Seen through Synagoggles," in *Judge,* vol. 2 (1882), No. 44, p. 10.

46. *Ibid.*

47. *West Point Tic Tacs,* New York: 1878, p. 69.

48. *Puck,* vol. 13 (1883), p. 68.

49. *Yankee Notions,* vol. 11 (1862), p. 131.

50. *War Letters of a Disbanded Volunteer . . .,* New York: 1864, p. 25.

51. *Life,* vol. 1 (1883), p. 281.

52. Shillaber, P. P., *Life and sayings of Mrs. Partington . . .,* New York: 1854, p. 237.

53. *The Post-Chaise Companion . . .,* Baltimore: 1830, by Clio Convivius, p. 144.

54. *Horn's Last* [no year], p. 14.

55. *Puck,* vol. 22 (1887/88), p. 286.

56. *Bill Nye's Red Book,* Chicago [1891], p. 160.

57. *Little Hill's Yankee Story Book,* Philadelphia [1836], p. 42.

58. Quire, Harry S., *Wall Street in Paradise . . .,* New York: 1869.

59. McLure, I. B., *Entertaining Anecdotes,* Chicago: 1881, p. 245.

60. *Puck,* vol. 12 (1882/83), p. 220.

61. Rev. Titus Joslin, *Centennial Skyrockets,* Albany: 1875, p. 71.

62. *Comic Annual* (H. P. Finn), Illustrations by D. C. Johnson [1831], p. 96.

63. *Judge,* vol. 5 (1883), No. 126, p. 12.

64. "Riddling Forest," in *Evenings in New England . . . By an American Lady,* Boston: 1824, p. 24.

65. "London Table Talks," in *Spirit of the Times,* vol. 6 (1836/37), pp. 244, 282.

66. Avery S. P., *The Harp of Thousand Strings . . .,* Nev [1858], p. 226.

67. White, Richard Grant, "American Pronunciation of English," *The Galaxy*, vol. 21 (1876), p. 529.

68. *Puck*, vol. 10 (1881/82), p. 164.

69. *Puck*, vol. 36 (1894/95), p. 74.

70. [James W. Morris], *K. N. Pepper* . . ., New York: 1859, pp. 193–199.

71. "The aristocracy of locality," in *Puck*, vol. 31 (1892), p. 294.

72. *Puck*, vol. 21 (1887), p. 385.

73. *Puck*, vol. 26 (1889/90), p. 440.

74. "Proverbs and Portraits, or Life on the Alaska," in *California Mail Bag*, vol. 2 (1872), p. 74.

75. *Letterbook of John Watts* . . ., New York: 1928, p. 288.

76. Watts, p. 385.

77. "Our Popular Farces. Our Relief Societies. Reported by Ed," in *The Judge*, vol. 1 (1881/82), No. 7, p. 7.

78. "Wayside Gushings. By Mrs. Harris," in *California Mailbag*, vol. 2 (1872), No. 2, p. 60.

79. *Puck*, vol. 4 (1878/79), No. 94, p. 1.

NOTES FOR CHAPTER 7

1. *Puck*, vol. 29 (1891), p. 362.

2. *Puck*, vol. 24 (1888/89), p. 202.

3. *Puck*, vol. 24 (1888/89), p. 214.

4. *Puck*, vol. 24 (1888/89), p. 327.

5. *Life*, vol. 3 (1884), p. 94.

6. *The Judge*, vol. 1 (1881/82), No. 3, p. 5.

7. *Puck*, vol. 24 (1888/89), p. 404.

8. *Puck*, vol. 24 (1888/89), p. 117.

9. *Puck*, vol. 21 (1887), p. 132.

10. Caricature by F. W. Read in *"Life,"* in *American Wit and Humor*, New York: 1907, Vol. I, p. 326.

11. *Puck*, vol. 27 (1890), p. 102.

12. *Puck*, vol. 25 (1889), p. 226.

13. *Vogue*, vol. 1 (1892/93), p. 306.

14. *Puck*, vol. 26 (1889/90), p. 37.

15. *Puck*, vol. 21 (1887), p. 371.

16. *Portland Figaro*, vol. 2 (1891), No. 43, p. 7.

17. *Puck*, vol. 24 (1888/89), p. 365.

18. Eduard Fuchs, *Die Juden in der Karikatur*, München: 1921, p. 104.

19. "A Philosopher," in *Flying Leaves* [18–], p. 13, but a ducat in "A clever infant," *Puck*, vol. 47 (1900), No. 1204, p. 7: "He von't trust a pank so quvick!"

20. *Puck*, vol. 48 (1900/1901), No. 1224, p. 11.

21. M. A. Woolf, *Sketches of lowly life, in a great city*, New York: 1889, p. 73.

22. *Puck,* vol. 47 (1900), No. 1216, p. 3.
23. *Puck,* vol. 39 (1896), No. 996, p. 3.
24. "Would fill the bill," in *Puck,* vol. 49 (1901), No. 1250, p. 3.
25. *"Chips' " Dogs. A collection of humorous drawings by* F. P. W. Bellew, Cartoon No. 9, 1895.
26. *Puck,* vol. 5 (1879), p. 116.
27. *Puck,* vol. 12 (1882/83), p. 292.
28. *Portland Figaro,* vol. 2 (1891), No. 45, p. 7.

NOTES FOR CHAPTER 8

1. *Puck Kalender 1883,* pp. 34–40.
2. "Summer Saunterings" III in *Life,* vol. 6 (1885), p. 103.
3. William Murrell, *A History of American Graphic Humor,* New York: 1933, vol. 2, p. 108.
4. "The Crossing Sweeper in Office—No. 7" in *The Spirit of the Times,* vol. 20 (1850/51), p. 507.
5. *Puck,* vol. 9 (1881), p. 116.
6. *Puck,* vol. 9 (1881), p. 60.
7. *Puck,* vol. 26 (1889/90), p. 182.
8. *Vogue,* vol. 1 (1892/93), p. 296.
9. Rudolf Glanz, *The Jews in American Alaska* (1867–1880), New York: 1953.
10. *Life,* vol. 41 (1903), p. 372.
11. *Life,* vol. 38 (1901), p. 195.
12. *Life,* vol. 22 (1893), pp. 412/13.
13. *Life,* vol. 27 (1896), p. 350, sgd. "Metcalfe."
14. "Mr. Frohman's Imposition," in *Life,* vol. 37 (1901), p. 416.
15. *Life,* vol. 40 (1902), p. 374.
16. *Life,* vol. 28 (1896), pp. 340/41.
17. *Life,* vol. 60 (1912), p. 1805.
18. *Life,* vol. 39 (1902), p. 2.
19. *"The French Maid," "The Kosher Vendetta,"* in *Life,* vol. 30 (1897), p. 292.
20. "A cable car conversazione," in *Life,* vol. 29 (1897), p. 236; also caricatures of Jews selling tickets in *Life,* vol. 35 (1900), pp. 272/73.
21. "An impressive performance" in *Life,* vol. 38 (1901), pp. 390/91.
22. *Life,* vol. 35 (1900), p. 213.
23. *Life,* vol. 27 (1896), pp. 11/12.
24. *Life,* vol. 27 (1896), p. 232.
25. *See* note 20.
26. *Life,* vol. 30 (1897), p. 418.
27. "A First Night," in *Life,* vol. 36 (1900), p. 349.
28. "The Profesh," in *Life,* vol. 32 (1898), pp. 93/94.
29. *See* note 20.
30. *Life,* vol. 27 (1901), p. 72.
31. *The Judge,* vol. 5 (1883), No. 113.

32. *Life,* vol. 38 (1901), pp. 210/11.

33. *Life,* vol. 45 (1905), p. 330. Weber and Shields, the important impersonators of Jews are caricatured in *Life,* vol. 38, p. 412.

34. *Jewish Messenger,* vol. 51 (1882), No. 19, p. 1: "A fellow named Frank Bush is disgracing himself and his profession by playing . . . Jew Specialties. . . ."

35. Mr. L'Arronge as Kalchas was exceedingly funny and we would deem him ideal in this role if he would only push a little less to the foreground the "Judischen Geheimen Ober-Rabbiner" (Jewish secret chief rabbi).

36. "An old yarn with the little 'Uns, in *The Spirit of the Times,"* vol. 21 (1851/52), p. 505.

NOTES FOR CHAPTER 9

1. *Life,* vol. 38 (1901), p. 354.

2. Cartoon "Bad for business," in *Puck,* vol. 39 (1896), No. 994, p. 1.

3. "Our Japanese Village," in *Puck,* vol. 18 (1885/86), pp. 312/313.

4. Cartoon "The national honor and credit in good hands," *Puck,* vol. 34 (1893/94), pp. 408/9.

5. Cartoon "An unequal contest; they can find no flaw in his armor," whereas the humorist finds the flaw in Pulitzer's Jewish status symbols of hat and spear, in *Puck,* vol. 45, No. 1168, pp. 8/9.

6. Cartoon "The wall of the Jingos," in *Puck,* vol. 37 (1895), pp. 8/9.

7. Cartoon "Busted," in *Puck,* vol. 46 (1899/1900), No. 1189, pp. 8/9.

8. *Life,* vol. 29 (1897), p. 215; *see also* the anti-Pulitzer cartoon "At last" in *Life,* vol. 29 (1897), pp. 358/59.

9. *Puck,* vol. 26 (1889/90), p. 140.

10. *Puck,* vol. 38 (1895/96), p. 401.

11. *Puck,* vol. 18 (1885/86), pp. 120/21.

12. *Puck,* vol. 30 (1891/92), pp. 184/85.

13. *Puck,* vol. 22 (1887/88), pp. 164/65.

14. *Puck,* vol. 22 (1887/88), pp. 378/9.

15. *Puck,* vol. 21 (1887), p. 253.

16. *Puck,* vol. 18 (1885/86), pp. 152/53.

17. *Puck,* vol. 43 (1898/99), No. 1113, p. 1.

18. *Puck,* vol. 39 (1896), No. 1011, pp. 8–9.

19. *Puck,* vol. 21 (1887), pp. 148/49.

20. "The national political mad-house," in *Puck,* vol. 22, (1887/88), pp. 24/25; "Another sort of presidential trip," in *Puck,* vol. 22 (1887/88), pp. 108/109; "Her true knight," in *Puck,* vol. 21 (1887), pp. 10/11; "The Medium and his dupes," in *Puck,* vol. 21 (1887), p. 89; "The good old time of 1886," in *Puck,* vol. 19 (1886), p. 181; "A large contract for three small boys," in *Puck,* vol. 21 (1887), p. 204; "Too solid to be smashed," p. 285; "Grand presidential auction sale for the year 1888," pp. 404/405; "Honor to McKinley!" in *Puck,* vol. 43 (1898), No. 1098, p. 1; "Pulitzus Mundanus," in *Life,* vol. 32 (1898).

21. *Puck,* vol. 39 (1896), No. 1002, p. 16.

22. *Puck,* vol. 39 (1896), No. 1004, pp. 8/9.

23. Quoted from James Wyman Barret, *Joseph Pulitzer and his World,* New York: 1941; pp. 73, 105, 109.

24. *Puck,* vol. 23 (1888), p. 181.

25. *Puck,* vol. 5 (1879), p. 53.

26. *F. H. T. Bellew—Caricaturist and Illustrator,* New York Public Library [1932]; Fifth Avenue Journal, 1872, "Fr. Bellew's Cartoon No. 1." Another caricature in this collection is "Mr. Pic endorses the governor," inscribed "G. J. Pick."

27. *Puck,* vol. 24 (1888/89), pp. 184/85.

28. *Life,* vol. 12 (1888), p. 39.

29. *Puck,* vol. 25 (1889), pp. 216/17.

30. *Puck,* vol. 26 (1889/90), p. 29.

31. *Twinkles,* New York, vol. 1 (1896/97), No. 18, p. 10.

32. *Life,* vol. 17 (1891), p. 213.

33. "The European Snarl," in *Puck,* vol. 3 (1878), No. 58.

34. *Puck,* vol. 1 (1876), No. 1, September 1876.

NOTES FOR CHAPTER 10

1. Harvard Theatre Collection, *Humbugs' American Museum,* New York, No. 3, August 1851, p. 10.

2. *Puck,* vol. 8 (1880/81), p. 339.

3. *The Judge,* vol. 2 (1882), No. 34, pp. 8–9.

4. *Puck,* vol. 7 (1880), pp. 130/31.

5. *Puck,* vol. 11 (1882), p. 244.

6. *Puck,* vol. 12 (1882/83), p. 287.

7. *The Household Book of Wit and Humor,* Philadelphia: 1883, p. 201.

8. *Puck,* vol. 29 (1891), p. 246.

9. *Life,* vol. 39 (1902), pp. 90/91.

10. *Puck,* vol. 49 (1901), No. 1257, p. 8.

11. *The Judge,* vol. 1 (1882), No. 22, p. 16.

12. *The Judge,* vol. 1 (1882), No. 23, p. 5.

13. *Puck,* vol. 11 (1882), p. 255, ". . . didn't you see how dem Rooshian Shoos got avay mit dose policemans in Gastle Garden? Don't dot vas gourage."

14. *Puck,* vol. 5 (1879/80), p. 291.

15. *Ibid.*

16. *Ibid.,* pp. 296/97.

17. *Mr. Dooley in Peace and War,* Boston: 1898, p. 55.

18. *Puck,* vol. 26 (1889/90), p. 302.

19. *Puck,* vol. 42 (1897/98), No. 1068, pp. 8/9.

20. *Puck,* vol. 34 (1893/94), p. 148.

21. *Life,* vol. 22 (1892), p. 366.

22. Wallace Irvin, *At the Sign of the Dollar,* New York: 1905, p. 56.

23. *Puck,* vol. 11 (1881/82), p. 248.

24. *Puck,* vol. 32 (1892/93), pp. 334/35, 338.

25. *Puck,* vol. 32 (1892/93), p. 422.

NOTES FOR CHAPTER 11

1. Cartoon "Uncle Sam's Lodging House," in *Puck,* vol. 11 (1882), pp. 220/21.

2. *Judge,* vol. 3 (1882/83), pp. 7–8.

3. *Puck,* vol. 30 (1891/92), p. 22.

4. *Yankee Notions,* vol. 9 (1860), p. 156.

5. *Puck,* vol. 37 (1895), p. 395.

6. *Puck,* vol. 9 (1881), p. 326.

7. *Puck,* vol. 32 (1892/93), p. 331.

8. *Puck,* vol. 33 (1893), p. 374.

9. *Puck,* vol. 5 (1879), p. 346.

10. F. H. Cahill, *Rare Bits of Humor,* New York [1906], p. 81.

11. *Puck on Wheels,* No. 5 (1884), pp. 68–70.

12. "Much preferred," in T. J. Carey, *Irish yarns and witty sayings* ..., New York: 1902, p. 72.

13. F. H. Cahill, *Rare Bits of Humor,* New York: 1906, p. 18.

14. *Puck,* vol. 34 (1893/94), p. 315.

15. *Harper's Magazine,* vol. 32 (1865/66), p. 134 "Editor's Drawer."

16. *The Spirit of the Times,* vol. 10 (1840/41), p. 430, "Foreign Police."

17. Cartoon "The Craze of religious colonization," in *Puck,* vol. 5 (1879), p. 296/97.

18. *Puck,* vol. 36 (1894/95), p. 13.

NOTES FOR CHAPTER 12

1. *Puck,* vol. 15 (1884), p. 369.

2. *Puck,* vol. 17 (1895), p. 261.

3. Cartoon *Puck Illustrierte humoristische Wochenschrift,* vol. 9 (1884/85), pp. 648/49. Herbert Asbury "When New York was really wicked. V-Fences." in *New Yorker,* vol. 3 (Jan. 7, 1928), pp. 22–24.

4. *Puck,* vol. 17 (1885), pp. 264/65.

5. *Puck,* vol. 62 (1907/8), No. 1596, p. 1.

6. *Life,* vol. 1 (1883), p. 281.

7. John Lambert, *Travels through Canada and the United States ... 1806, 1807, 1808,* London: 1814, vol. 2, p. 106.

8. *Puck,* vol. 30 (1891/1892), p. 80.

9. *The American Jew,* New York: 1888, p. 7: "Look carefully before taking risks offered by men whose names end in ein, ky or kie. . . ."

10. Especially in the volumes of *Puck.*

11. *Puck,* vol. 43 (1898), No. 1117, p. 4.

12. *Puck,* vol. 38 (1895/96), p. 405.

13. *Puck*, vol. 43 (1898), No. 1117, p. 4.
14. *Puck*, vol. 40 (1896/97), No. 1027, p. 10.
15. *Puck*, vol. 36 (1894/95), pp. 232/33.
16. *Puck*, vol. 46 (1899/1900), No. 1175, p. 10.
17. *Puck*, vol. 39 (1896), No. 1012, p. 2.
18. *Puck*, vol. 41 (1897), No. 1056, p. 4.
19. *Puck*, vol. 40 (1896/97), No. 1031, p. 27.
20. *Puck*, vol. 46 (1899/1900), No. 1176, p. 10.
21. *Puck*, vol. 20 (1886/87), p. 127.
22. *Puck*, vol. 29 (1891), p. 167.
23. *Puck*, vol. 41 (1897), No. 1045, p. 10.
24. *Puck*, vol. 33 (1893), p. 26.
25. *Puck*, vol. 46 (1899/1900), No. 1182, p. 4.
26. *Puck*, vol. 36 (1894/95), p. 234.
27. *Life,* vol. 16 (1890), p. 288.
28. *Life,* vol. 25 (1895), p. 135.
29. *Puck,* vol. 51 (1902), No. 1306, p. 17.
30. *Life,* vol. 22 (1892), p. 165.

NOTES FOR CHAPTER 13

1. ". . . Der Heavenrich, Seasongood, Lion und Moses, Die fangen zusammen ein Kleiderg'schäft an; Nicht klein wie ein Dalfin, es gibt was ganz Grosses, Und werden immense Geschäfte getan. Auf einmal damacht die Mischboge Machulle, Die Gläubiger munkeln wohl dies und auch das, Und suchen, weil das was herauskommt, ist Nulle, Prozentchen dann mit dem Vergrösserungsglas." Richard Weinacht, *Carnevals Blüthen,* New York: 1886, p. 89 "Das Vergrösserungsglas."
2. *Der deutsche Pionier,* vol. 15 (1883/84), p. 327. "Herr Löwenstein und seine Pläne oder wie baut man seine Ritterburg." (Mr. Lowenstein and his plans or how one builds his knight's castle.")
3. *Der Sternenwirth, Humoristisch—Satirisches Brauerblatt,* "Offizielles Organ für amerikanischen Brauerhumor," vol. 2 (1892/93), p. 4.
"Des Vater Adam Gerstenbau—
Ernaehrte ihn und Sohn und Frau.
Doch Geld war keines zu verdienen,
Weil keine Händler noch erschienen.
Sonst wär gewesen g'rade er, —
Der erste jüdische Handelsherr."
4. *Der Sternenwirth,* vol. 2 (1892/93), p. 7.
5. *Der Sternenwirth,* vol. 2 (1892/93), p. 9.
6. *Der Sternenwirth,* vol. 2 (1892/93), p. 46.
". . . wie en Hoppenjud die Countrybrauerei wann er sein vorjaehrige vertrocknete Hoppe noch schnell loswerden will ehender de neie uff de Markt kommt."
7. ". . . lässt sich Braumeister schimpfen . . ." *Der Sternenwirth,* vol. 2, p. 28.

8. *Ibid.,* "Stätte jüdischer Schinderei."

9. *Ibid.,* "zwei schäbigen Judenjünglingen . . ." "Ich habe vieler Herren Länder gesehen, in ungezählten Brauereien angeschoben, ein einziges Mal auch bei einem Vertreter des Volkes Israel, der zu den gelungenten seines Stammes zählen dürfte.

Herr Salomon Ketzeles war ein fainer Mann, der früher hat gemacht in Hadern, Knochen und anderen Parfümerien, später wurde er auf Grund erworbener Kenntnisse Hopfenhändler und brachte es durch weises und vorsichtiges Geschäftsgebaren his zum Besitzer der Lerchenheimer Brauerei."

10. "Wer hat's Theater, hat die Kunst Von jeher unterstützt? Der vielverhöhnten Juden Gunst Hat gerne sie beschützt." (Richard Weinacht, *Carnevals Blüthen,* New York: 1886.)

NOTES FOR CHAPTER 14

1. *The Cartoon,* vol. 1 (1908) no longer shows any Jewish or other ethnic caricature.

2. *Harper's Magazine,* vol. 51 (1875), p. 199.

3. "Street Cries," in *Round Table,* vol. 3 (1866), p. 336.

4. *Atlantic Monthly,* vol. 25 (1870), pp. 199–204. Charles Dawson Shanly "The Street-Cries of New York," p. 203.

5. "Do the Americans wear old clothes?" in *The Literary World,* vol. 10 (1852), p. 106. Frank Weitenkampf, *Social History of the United States in Caricature,* New York: 1953, p. 61.

6. *Puck on Wheels,* No. 3, 1882, p. 15 "Dictionary."

7. *Ibid.,* pp. 82–87.

NOTES FOR CHAPTER 15

1. *Puck,* vol. 34 (1893/94), p. 266.

2. *Puck,* vol. 33 (1893), p. 194.

3. *Life,* vol. 14 (1889), p. 110.

4. *Puck,* vol. 36 (1894/95), p. 442.

5. *Puck,* vol. 11 (1882), p. 37.

6. "Puckographs—XXII. One of the Children of the Ghetto," in vol. 46 (1899/1900), No. 1180, p. 2. *Puck,* vol. 24 (1888/89), p. 263. "Not to be discouraged.—Ipstein.—Shoestrings, collar puttons, susbenders" picture.

7. *Puck,* vol. 5 (1879), p. 247.

8. *The Judge,* vol. 2, No. 32 (June 3, 1882), pp. 8–9.

9. *Puck,* vol. 4 (1878/79), No. 94, p. 1.

10. *Puck,* vol. 4 (1878/79), No. 94, p. 7.

11. *The Illustrated Dramatic Weekly,* New York, vol. 1 (1879), No. 8, p. 6.

12. W. A. Croffut, *Some Funny Bible Stories,* New York: 1812.

13. [Avery] *Mrs. Partington's Carpet Bag of Fun* . . ., New York: 1854, p. 51.

14. *Ibid.,* p. 285.

15. Oliver Herford, *An Alphabet of Celebrities,* Boston: 1899.

16. *Puck,* vol. 5 (1879), p. 304.

17. *Puck,* vol. 17 (1885), pp. 200/201.

18. *Die Fehme,* St. Louis, 1869/70, No. 15, p. 3.

19. *Puck,* vol. 29 (1891), p. 291.

20. "Suez Canal," in *Die Fehme,* No. 12, St. Louis, 1869/70.

21. One of them is: Newspaper Cartoonists Association of Cincinnati. Cincinnatians as we see them. Cincinnati 1905.

NOTES FOR CHAPTER 16

1. Henry Collins Brown. *New York of Yesterday* . . . New York: 1924, p. 38.

2. Mrs. Grundy, vol. 1, p. 94.

3. *Artemus Ward, his Book,* New York: 1864, p. 243.

4. *The Judge,* vol. 1 (1882), No. 24, p. 10.

5. *Puck,* vol. 25 (1889), p. 134.

6. *The Judge,* vol. 2, No. 37 (July 8, 1882), p. 3.

7. *Puck,* vol. 37 (1895), p. 36.

8. *Puck,* vol. 25 (1889), p. 166.

9. *Puck,* vol. 14 (1883/84), p. 4.

10. *Puck,* vol. 38 (1895/96), pp. 424/25.

11. *Puck,* vol. 29 (1891), p. 362.

12. *Life,* vol. 25 (1895), p. 108.

13. *Life,* vol. 38 (1901), p. 213.

14. *Life,* vol. 22 (1892), p. 172.

15. *Puck,* vol. 26 (1889/90), p. 169.

16. *Puck,* vol. 34 (1893/94), p. 357.

17. *The Judge,* vol. 2, No. 33 (July 10, 1882), pp. 8–9.

18. *Puck,* vol. 30 (1891/92), p. 70.

19. *Life,* vol. 14 (1889), p. 299.

20. *Life,* vol. 45 (1905), p. 222.

21. *Life,* vol. 30 (1897), p. 268.

22. *Life,* vol. 27 (1896), p. 291.

23. *Ibid.*

24. *Life,* vol. 61 (1913), p. 25.

25. *Life,* vol. 60 (1912), p. 2097.

26. "Wouldn't you like to be a famous actress, girlee?," in *Life,* vol. 60 (1912), p. 1907; *Life,* vol. 45 (1905), pp. 220, 253, 285, 307, 380, 386; "The Public be burned," 489.

27. "Isaac and his love for nature," in *Life,* vol. 35 (1900), p. 397.

28. *Life,* vol. 35 (1900), p. 541.

29. "Dinkelspiel takes a shy at Bridge Whist," in *Life,* vol. 45 (1905), p. 562.

30. *Life,* vol. 60 (1912), p. 1956.
31. *Life,* vol. 27 (1896), p. 81.
32. *Life,* vol. 16 (1890), p. 321.
33. Walt McDougall, *The Un-authorized History of Columbus,* Newark, p. 175.
34. *The Judge,* vol. 2 (1882), No. 39, pp. 8/9.
35. *Life,* vol. 58 (1911), p. 1124.
36. *Life,* vol. 26 (1895), p. 410.
37. *Life,* vol. 38 (1901), p. 272.
38. *Life,* vol. 40 (1902), p. 266.
39. "Kicker's Column," in *Life,* vol. 38 (1901), p. 314.
40. *Life,* vol. 27 (1896), p. 364.
41. *Life,* vol. 23 (1894), p. 100.
42. *Life,* vol. 21 (1893), p. 269.
43. *Life,* vol. 5 (1885), p. 271.
44. *Life,* vol. 15 (1890), p. 304 (turf-man and a Jew), a bet; vol. 8 (1886), p. 404 "Delicately put," an army anecdote.
45. *Life,* vol. 30 (1897), p. 315.
46. "The last Christian sign," in *The Judge,* vol. 2 (1882), No. 48, p. 2.
47. *The Judge,* vol. 1 (1881/82), No. 22, p. 16.
48. *The Judge,* vol. 2 (1882), No. 27, p. 2, cartoon pp. 8/9.
49. *The Judge,* vol. 2 (1882), No. 40, p. 6.
50. *The Judge,* vol. 3 (1882/83), No. 59, p. 2.
51. *Puck,* vol. 11 (1882), p. 156.

NOTES FOR CHAPTER 17

1. "Our St. Louis Letter," in *Jewish Messenger,* vol. 57 (1885), No. 9, p. 5.
2. "Lone Star Flashes," in *American Israelite,* vol. 29 (1882), p. 66.
3. *Puck,* vol. 8 (1880/81), pp. 228/29.
4. *Puck,* vol. 8 (1880/81), pp. 228/29.

CONCLUSIONS

1. Thomas L. Masson. *Our American Humorists,* New York: 1922, p. 136.
2. Masson, p. 135.
3. *Harper's Magazine,* vol. 50 (1874), pp. 690–701 "American Humor," p. 698.
4. Joe Chandler Harris, *American Wit and Humor,* New York: 1901, Introduction.

APPENDIX

1. *The American Jest Book . . .,* Harrisburg: 1796, p. 20.
2. *The Watchtower,* Cooperstown, vol. 5 (1818/19), Feb. 1, 1819, p. 4.

3. *Frank Leslie's Chimney-corner,* vol. 7 (1868), p. 352.

4. *Nix Nax,* New York, vol. 6 (1861), p. 237.

5. *Harper's Magazine,* vol. 30 (1864/65), p. 131.

6. *Harper's Bazaar,* vol. 2, p. 672.

7. *Woodhill and Claffin's Weekly,* vol. 1, No. 3 (May 28, 1870), p. 6.

8. "A time to flabbergast," in *Nix Nax,* New York, vol. 4 (1859), p. 81.

9. *Everybody's Magazine,* vol. 18 (1908), p. 285.

10. R. Glisan, *Journal of Army Life,* San Francisco: 1874, p. 184. (Entry dated April 26, 1855.)

11. "Salmigundi," in *Southern Biwouac,* N. S. vol. 1 (1885/86), No. 3, p. 128.

12. *Spirit of the Times,* vol. 20 (1850/51), p. 85.

13. "Gossip with Readers and Correspondents," *Spirit of the Times,* vol. 23 (1853/54), p. 303.

14. *The Knickerbocker,* vol. 36 (1850), pp. 489–498; Richard Haywards, "On Wit and Humor," p. 491.

15. "Facetiae," in *Harper's Bazaar,* vol. 9 (1876), p. 352.

16. "Editor's Drawer. This comes to the Drawer from a Canadian friend" in *Harper's Magazine,* vol. 55 (1875/76), p. 478.

Index